General Editors: J. R. MULRYNE
and J. C. BULMAN
Associate Editor: Margaret Shewring

Henry IV, Part Two

Already published in the series

Volumes on most other plays in preparation

Of related interest

Shakespeare in Performance

Henry IV, Part Two

BARBARA HODGDON

Manchester University Press
Manchester and New York

Distributed exclusively in the USA and Canada by St. Martin's Press

Copyright © BARBARA HODGDON 1993

Published by
Manchester University Press
Oxford Road, Manchester M13 9PL, UK
and Room 400, 175 Fifth Avenue,
New York, NY 10010, USA

Distributed exclusively in the USA and Canada
by St. Martin's Press, Inc.,175 Fifth Avenue,
New York, NY 10010, USA

British Library cataloguing-in-publication data
A catalogue record for this book is available
from the British Library

Library of Congress cataloging-in-publication data
Hodgdon, Barbara, 1932–
    Henry IV, part two / Barbara Hodgdon.
        p.   cm. — (Shakespeare in performance)
    Includes bibliographical references and index.
    ISBN 0-7190-2751-9.
    1. Shakespeare, William, 1564-1616. King Henry IV. Part 2.
2. Henry IV, King of England, 1367–1413, in fiction, drama, poetry,etc.
3. Shakespeare, William 1564–1616—Stage history—1950-
4. Great Britain—History—Henry IV, 1399–1413—Historiography.
5. Kings and rulers in literature. I. Title. II. Series.
PR2811.H55   1993
822.3'3—dc20   92-31594

ISBN 0 7190 2751 9 *hardback*

Typeset by
Koinonia Limited, Manchester
Printed in Great Britain
by Biddles Limited, Guildford and King's Lynn

CONTENTS

The illustrations appear between chapters v and vi, pp. 118, 119

SERIES EDITORS' PREFACE

The study of Shakespeare's plays as scripts for performance in the theatre has grown in recent years to become a major interest for many university, college and secondary-school students and their teachers. The aim of the present series is to assist this study by describing how certain of Shakespeare's texts have been realised in production.

The series is not concerned to provide theatre histories. Rather, each contributor has selected a small number of productions of a particular play and studied them comparatively. The productions, often from different periods, countries and media, have been chosen because they are significant interpretations in their own right, but also because they represent something of the range and variety of possible interpretations of the play in hand. We hope that students and theatregoers, by reading these accounts of Shakespeare in performance, may enlarge their understanding of the text and begin, too, to appreciate some of the ways in which practical considerations influence the meanings a production incorporates: the stage the actor plays on, the acting company, the player's own physique and abilities, stage-design and theatre-tradition, as well as the political, social and economic conditions of performance and the expectations of a particular audience.

Any study of a Shakespeare text will reveal only a small proportion of the text's potential meaning. We hope that the effect of this series will be to encourage a kind of reading that is receptive to the ever-varying discoveries theatre interpretation provides.

J. R. Mulryne
J. C. Bulman
Margaret Shewring

ACKNOWLEDGEMENTS

Sylvia Morris, Marian Pringle and Mary White of the Library at the Shake-speare Centre in Stratford provided prompt copies and other materials and made working at the Centre a distinctive pleasure. Christopher Robinson at the Theatre Collection of the University of Bristol helped by telling me what was not available; and Sue Evans of the English Shakespeare Company graciously permitted me to see an 'in-process' prompt copy and a number of photographs. I am grateful to the Drake University Center for the Human-ities for funding travel expenses and for a semester's research leave. James Bulman offered extremely expert critical and editorial advice at several stages of writing, and his fellow editor, J. R. Mulryne, gave the manuscript a meticulous review. Among the colleagues and friends who responded to questions, provided information, and offered prompt and willing advice, I would especially like to mention Lynda Boose, Samuel Crowl, Miriam Gilbert, Lorraine Helms, Sarah Lyons, Philip McGuire, Scott McMillin and Peter Saccio. As always, Richard Abel's encouragement and loving support enriches theatregoing, writing and everyday life.

Some 'thick descriptions' and arguments rework those in *The End Crowns All: Closure and Contradiction in Shakespeare's History*; my thanks to Princeton University Press for permission to use this material. Per-mission to reproduce photographs has been kindly granted by the Shakespeare Birthplace Trust, Laurence Burns, Chris Davies, Mig Holte and Angus McBean.

All references are to the Oxford Shakespeare: *William Shakespeare, The Complete Works*, edited by Stanley Wells and Gary Taylor (1986).

B. H.

CHAPTER I

Introduction

I

Spectators at the first performances of *2 Henry IV* would have experienced a play that differed, in at least one respect, from its later configurations. That play would have been framed by two dramatic conventions: an Induction spoken by the figure of Rumour 'painted full of tongues' and an Epilogue, according to some editors, spoken by a dancer (*Ind.*, s.d.; *Ep.*, s.d.). Familiar to late Elizabethan audiences as markers for theatrical fictions, these framing conventions are either transformed (Rumour) or absent (the Epilogue) in the productions discussed in this volume. While neither change has such immediate and far-reaching implications for present-day performance as the inclusion or omission of the Christopher Sly material in *The Taming of the Shrew* (see Graham Holderness's volume in this series), both offer evidence of a particular intersection between the theatrical event and its cultural context that gave *2 Henry IV*'s first performances an exclusively 'local habitation'.

Some members of those heterogeneous late Elizabethan audiences would have identified Rumour as the emblematic embodiment of Fame, a figure with classical origins common in both sixteenth-century literary and theatrical cultures: in 1553, for instance, the Revels Office records payment for a coat and cap for Fame to be painted with eyes, tongues and ears. Indeed, Rumour's first words, 'Open your ears', point to one probable distinction separating late Elizabethan and present-day theatrical practices – that between a primarily oral/aural and a primarily visual culture. Where a single figure acting as the play's 'presenter' once began the play, twentieth-century productions tend to turn the Induction into a spectacle, either (as in Michael Redgrave's 1951 production) by making Rumour's figure the centre of an elaborate dumb-show representing the aftermath of the Shrewsbury battle in *Part One* or (as in Terry Hands's 1975 production) splitting the speech among a number of black-clad actors who literally *embody* the textual stage direction's 'full of tongues'. Although such stagings can be seen as attempts to mediate between Elizabethan dramatic conventions and present-day cultures, late sixteenth-century and twentieth-century audiences can also be supposed to share some understanding of rumour as a social practice. Then as now, rumour has considerable power to manipulate individual reputation (Iago dramatises an extreme case), to further political or social ambitions, to solidify a particular group's sense of itself and to measure, in Lear's words, 'Who loses and who wins; who's in, who's out' (V.ii.15; see Spacks, pp. 3-23). Both audiences would probably associate rumour with idle talk and ambiguous facts and interpretations. But while late sixteenth-century anti-theatrical commentators might also link Rumour's emphasis on false report to the dangers of theatrical culture in general, present-day critics tend to view the Induction as entirely appropriate to a play which exploits historical facts as theatrical fiction and which, primarily though not exclusively through Falstaff, suggests that history, like theatre, is a compellingly convenient illusion. 'Is not the truth the truth?' asks Falstaff (*1 Henry IV*, II.v.233-4), posing the issues Rumour raises more directly. It depends on who tells the story.

Like twentieth-century spectators, Elizabethan audiences probably would have anticipated Falstaff's return in a play called *Henry IV, Part Two* as much as they might have imagined, based on their experience of Shakespeare's earlier histories, that such a play would dramatise Hal's succession as Henry V. But their expectations about Falstaff's return would also have been coloured by topical rumours that had sparked considerable notoriety. In *1 Henry IV*'s first performances, Falstaff had been called Oldcastle, a name Shakespeare borrowed from a character in *The Famous Victories of Henry V*, an anonymous play which served as one narrative source for both *Henry* plays. But that name also connected the character to an historical Sir John Oldcastle, a Protestant martyr who had been sentenced to death for treason by Henry V and whose life was celebrated in Foxe's *Actes and Monuments*; and his sixteenth-century descendants – one was Sir William Brooke, the Lord Chamberlain, with responsibilities for overseeing the Master of the Revels and the licensing of plays – objected strenuously to what they saw as libellous comic parody of a worthy ancestor. The matter was sensitive enough that Shakespeare changed the name, and *2 Henry IV*'s Epilogue not only promises another play 'with Sir John in it' but calls attention to the fact that Falstaff is Oldcastle in *Part One* and Falstaff in *Part Two*: 'Where, for any thing I know, Falstaff shall die of a sweat – unless already a be kill'd with your hard opinions. For Oldcastle died a martyr, and this is not the man' (*Ep*. 27-30). The subject of anecdotes, letters, and rival plays, the Oldcastle–Falstaff controversy may well have been fuelled by the character's impersonator, the famous clown, Will Kemp, whom Thomas Nashe described as 'jest-monger and Vice-regent general to the ghost of Dick Tarlton' and who 'succeeded' Tarlton as a favourite of Queen Elizabeth as well as the general public. David Wiles argues persuasively that the Oldcastle–Falstaff role was written with Kemp in mind and that Kemp's particular skills helped to shape it: known for his ability to produce the illusion of spur-of-the-moment improvisation, he was also famous for his dancing, to which the Epilogue refers. Furthermore, the conventions which coded a clown's role – especially ambiguous social status, semi-androgynous identity, and his freedom to comment on other characters through direct address – agree quite precisely with Falstaff's attributes (pp. 11, 116-20).

In its late Elizabethan configuration, then, the play concluded much as it had begun, by interweaving 'truth' and 'false report' to allay historical rumour (the Oldcastle matter) and incite fresh theatrical rumour (a new Falstaff play). Understandably, the Epilogue has rarely been spoken since Shakespeare's day. Although W. Bridges-Adams's 1932 Stratford production included it – perhaps both to acknowledge the author's 'complete text' and to compliment the Prince of Wales, who attended the birthday performance but left long before the Epilogue was spoken (Beauman, *Royal Shakespeare*, pp. 114-20) – the history it traces has faded. That history points to negotiations between late Elizabethan theatrical companies and governmental licensing authorities that have present-day counterparts, especially in terms of censorship of and funding for the arts. Today, however, such controversies are played out not on the stages of public theatres, which served Elizabethan audiences as a new form of mass communication, but in the daily press.

Late Elizabethan spectators would have brought to *2 Henry IV* other items of cultural baggage that, while perhaps less remote than the matters alluded to in the Epilogue, still go beyond the general and obvious differences that mark off Elizabethan from twentieth-century theatrical circumstances. They would, for example, have had specifically local reference points for the Boar's Head tavern: at least six real taverns of that name existed in Elizabethan London, and one had been converted into a playhouse. Situated outside the City limits in Whitechapel, this Boar's Head had taprooms, four parlours for meals or private parties, and eleven bedrooms (Gurr, pp. 117-19); one of several inns of questionable status, it was part bar, part brothel, and part playhouse, combining in one venue the disorderly, time-wasting pleasures that Puritan commentators found most dangerously troubling and wished to censor. Shakespeare's Boar's Head is just such an ambiguous locale. In *Part One*, it is the site of a playlet that degrades royalty by aping it; *Part Two* dramatises its function as a brothel; and in both, Hal is seen 'play[ing] practical jokes and rubb[ing] elbows with a dissolute crew whose social rank is far beneath his own ... behav[ing], in short, like an aristocrat at an Elizabethan public theatre' (Rackin, p. 104). Although such a precise historical connection between tavern and playhouse is less available to present-day audiences, productions suggest that the tavern where Falstaff holds court is a disreputable place primarily by mapping that shame on the bodies of Mistress Quickly and Doll Tearsheet, who are often portrayed as a recognisably Victorian bourgeois madam and her prize whore. Such misogyny, it appears, is the only vital sign of the complex web of social relations that once linked debasement with theatrical culture.

One register of meaning twentieth-century performance can and does convey is that the Falstaff of *2 Henry IV* has achieved (if only through his own rumours, or lies) a new prosperity, and costume becomes the sign of this in all the productions discussed in this volume. But Elizabethan spectators would have had an even more precise understanding of Falstaff's cash and credit problems, his status as a prodigal father and his inflated sense of value. When Falstaff asks the Lord Chief Justice for £1,000 to 'furnish [him] forth' (I.iii.225), he is requesting approximately half the average

[4]

income of a noble or well-to-do member of the merchant bour-
geoisie; the price of the short cloak and slops (£30–£60) he has
ordered from Master Dommelton would far exceed the wages of an
artisan (6s per week) or schoolmaster (£15 per year); in 1597,
Shakespeare purchased the deed to Stratford's New Place for £60.
The 'seven groats and two pence' (I.iii.236) in his purse would
purchase several seats at a public or private theatre, even to enjoy
the luxury of a lord's room (approximately 6d); but that amount
was closer to a soldier's daily food allowance than to the rising
costs of English beef or to sack, which Falstaff prefers to beer (at 2/
3 gallon for a penny). He would borrow £10 from Mistress Quickly
– some indication of her success as a businesswoman and a sum
she cannily attempts to reduce to a third of £1; yet neither amount
would go far to purchase Doll the kirtle and cap Falstaff promises,
at a time when gowns ranged from £7 to £20 apiece (Gurr, pp. 12-
13, 178). No other *history* play so clearly sketches in details of late
sixteenth-century standards of 'getting and spending'; in this, *2
Henry IV* anticipates the later city comedies by Middleton and others,
where flesh itself goes up for sale and where spectators would encounter figures who, like Falstaff, indulge in or scramble for the fat
pleasures of pre-capitalist culture. Not only would Falstaff's situation
as a knight without landed property be familiar in a culture where
spending power was beginning to be defined in terms of cash value,
but so would those of *2 Henry IV*'s invisible characters – Master
Tisick, the deputy; Master Dumbe, the minister; the physician who
reads Falstaff's water; and Master Dommelton, the tailor – whose
names and occupations figure a world of commodity enterprise
and changing class status just off the limits of the stage. To the
extent that spectators could see, in Falstaff's inflationary spending,
in Poins's aspirations (which included marrying his sister to Prince
Hal), in Quickly's refusal to pawn both her plate and tapestries and
in Shallow's quick adage, 'a friend i'th'court is better than a penny
in the purse' (V.i.26-7), their own socio-economic strivings, *2 Henry
IV* was clearly dramatising *contemporary* history.

The play also dramatises, in its royal narrative, an historical
past, and it is the theatre that mediates the collision between that
history and the Elizabethan present, shaping both to its own
demands to stage what could be called a *double history*. If, as some
scholars claim, the Elizabethan age was in the process not only of
recognising and giving new weight to 'the pastness of the past' but
also of constructing a 'new' historiography different from Christian

providential history, then one way in which *2 Henry IV* contributed to that debate was by calling history, as a category, into question. Certainly Rumour raises the possibility of misrepresenting 'history'; and in some sense, *2 Henry IV* turns history into a theatrical commodity. One Elizabethan spectator, Thomas Nashe, saw a direct relationship between 'the Personator' and 'the man Personated'; unlike *written* historical records, staged history could make the past present: moreover, it 'hath power to new-mold the hearts of the spectators and fashion them to the shape of any noble and notable attempt' (*Apology*, B4r). In Nashe's terms, such 'fashioning' generated a specifically *masculine* valour which, in the waning decade of Queen Elizabeth's reign, had considerable ideological import. Although Elizabeth had consistently used the image of masculinity as a figure for her royal person and had represented herself as both male and female, as prince or honorary male and as England's mother and lover, she was an anomaly in an age that considered men the ideal leaders. As the sixteenth century ended, not only was Elizabeth's power declining but she had, as yet, named no heir; although James VI of Scotland was thought by many to be the logical choice, the succession issue remained a matter of anxious debate. And in staging a series of historical dramas, all of which produce male rulers, the theatre participated in this cultural work of re-masculinising England.

Admittedly, some of these concerns are speculative. Yet they do raise a series of issues that have equally ideological implications for present-day productions of Shakespeare's English history plays. While late Elizabethan spectators presumably experienced what I earlier called a double history, twentieth-century audiences are likely to experience a performance that collapses the two into a unitary historical past, a theatricalised 'Elizabethanism'. Some productions attempt to reify a lost Elizabethan past through choices of *mise-en-scène* that produce the illusion of direct access to an historical period; some rely on evoking the staging conventions of the Elizabethan theatre; some do both. Almost invariably, the souvenir programmes for present-day productions attempt to shore up spectators' understanding by reproducing texts and illustrations from the period as well as including snippets from recent critical and historical commentaries: more often than not, these contain clues to a production's particular emphases and its angle of vision. One production, staged by the English Shakespeare Company, made design decisions that effectively recreated the collision between historical periods that contributed to late sixteenth-century spectators' experience of double history. While many reviewers objected to the production's fluid negotiation among historical particulars, others saw this as an important corrective to the nostalgic bent of other stagings. Where Nashe once saw staged history making the past live in the eternal present of Elizabethan theatrical culture, what seems most important in twentieth-century productions (the ESC's excluded) is *preserving* that Elizabethan past. Herein lies the peculiar value of present-day productions: each appropriates 'Shakespeare-history' to make contact with, reproduce, and explore the historical past – perhaps hoping, as Terry Eagleton writes, 'to find some alternative to the nightmare of 'history'' (p. 30). Although in some ways this repeated revival has analogies with the late sixteenth-century succession debate, each present-day production also creates a different and historically specific cultural map of English, and Shakespearian, history.

II

As *1 Henry IV*'s tavern playlet breaks off with Hal's promise to banish Falstaff ('I do. I will') and the arrival of a court messenger, Falstaff says, 'Play out the play! I have much to say in the behalf of that [Falstaff]' (*1 Henry IV*, II.v.486; 489-90). Since *2 Henry IV* certainly affords him that opportunity, his words offer one way of imagining the serial relationship of *Part One* and *Part Two*, long a matter of critical conjecture. Were the *Henrys* conceived as one big play, or did Shakespeare plan, from the outset, to write a two-part play? One compositional myth proposes that both were concurrently under way; yet another writes a history of authorial failure in which Shakespeare, finding too much material for a single play, chopped it in half and fleshed out *Part Two*'s meagre historical events with the fictional Falstaff. Both explanations rely on an anecdote (or rumour) that accounts for *The Merry Wives of Windsor* appearing between *Parts One* and *Two*. Shakespeare, so the story goes, dropped his work on *Part Two* in order to obey Queen Elizabeth's desire to see a play about 'Sir John in love', returning to it later. A more theatrical (and commercial) explanation assumes that *Part Two* was written in order to capitalise on Faltaff's popularity: then as now, as the Epilogue's teasing promise of a new Falstaff play suggests, box-office success counted for something.

Although Philip Henslowe's diary records that the Admiral's

Men, rivals to Shakespeare's company, the Lord Chamberlain's Men, presented two-part plays at successive performances in 1594, 1595 and 1596, no evidence either confirms or denies that *1* and *2 Henry IV* were performed sequentially in Shakespeare's time. By contrast, the way in which twentieth-century spectators have most usually experienced the *Henrys* is by seeing them performed as a two-part play, or as part of a trilogy (with *Henry V*) or a tetralogy that includes *Richard II* as well as *Henry V*; in several cases, they have even appeared at the centre of a cycle of plays beginning with *Richard II* and ending with *Richard III*. Such constructs or frameworks, which show the influence of literary scholarship on theatrical production, would have been accessible only to those late Elizabethan spectators who could afford to attend the theatre regularly and who would, across months and sometimes years of theatregoing, have seen all the plays. While present-day productions sometimes run consecutively, making it possible to see a trilogy of plays in a day or, in the case of larger cycles, to attend a marathon weekend, Elizabethans could experience historical drama chronologically only as *readers*. By 1600, both *Henrys* had been published in Quarto, but it was not until the Folio was published in 1623 that readers could experience the plays not just as a serial two-part drama but as part of a much larger sequence of plays concerning English history.

If Nashe's comments can be taken as representative of a late sixteenth-century appetite for history, and *2 Henry IV*'s Epilogue as evidence of Falstaff's success, one might conjecture that late Elizabethan performances of *2 Henry IV* struck a balance between history and Falstaff's story. By the time of its post-Restoration revivals, however, *2 Henry IV*, like *1 Henry IV*, had become a Falstaff play. Judging from a 1662 engraving of Shakespearian characters (later used as the frontispiece for Francis Kirkman's *The Wits, or Sport upon Sport* [1672]), Falstaff was already being regentrified to suit the fashion of the times: he wears a slim rapier rather than a sword, his doublet sports a lace collar and cuffs, his half-boots are stylishly turned down and he carries a huge goblet; beside him stands Mistress Quickly, in a caricature of Puritan garb. Both stand at the front edge of a stage lit by candelabra and footlights and surrounded by spectators on three sides, with some seated in a gallery at the back of the stage. Whether or not their foreground stage position indicates their prominence, they are the only characters among seven others (all types of fools or clowns) who are identified by name. What appears to have been as true for seventeenth-century as for present-day productions is that performing either of the *Henrys* depended on whether a particular company had an available Falstaff, and the list of those who played the role up to 1900 encompasses many famous actors and actor–managers: William Cartwright, Thomas Betterton, James Quin, Stephen and Charles Kemble, R. W. Elliston, Samuel Phelps, James Hackett and Herbert Beerbohm Tree.

Centred on Falstaff, *2 Henry IV* became a markedly different play. Eighteenth-century revivals had little use for the Northumberland scenes (I.i; II.iii), which were cut both in Betterton's 1703 play and in John Bell's famous 1773 acting edition, reflecting current Drury Lane theatrical practice. Both also transposed Henry IV's soliloquy on sleep (III.i) to act as prologue to the crown scene (IV.v), one of several practical reorderings designed to make the play easier to handle on stages that were becoming increasingly pictorial (Odell, v. I, pp. 85-6; 243-4). Although similar cuts and rearrangements were not uncommon for the times, eighteenth- and nineteenth-century *2 Henry IV*s also revealed further traces of theatrical and cultural negotiation which, because they affected the play's ending, also affected Falstaff.

Betterton's fifth act, for instance, began with Falstaff's rejection (V.v) and continued into *Henry V*'s opening scenes, where the Lord Chief Justice and the Archbishop of Canterbury justify Henry V's claim to France (I.i); the French ambassador, led by Cambridge, Scroop and Grey, entered bearing the tennis balls (I.ii); and the play ended with Henry V's discovery of their treason and his orders for their execution (II.ii). Perhaps most obviously, Betterton's 'altered' play anticipates the trilogy connection that would become familiar to twentieth-century spectators. Yet it is also curiously Janus-faced. In so far as it models its ending on that of *1 Henry IV*, where, after Hal agrees to gild Falstaff's Shrewsbury lie, Henry IV sentences the Northern rebels to death, it softens Falstaff's rejection and makes Hal into a kinder, gentler monarch who gives limited prison sentences to clowns and reserves the death penalty for historical traitors. But in so far as it invites paralleling Falstaff with Cambridge, Scroop and Gray, it flirts with representing the newly crowned king as a tyrant. The simplest way of avoiding what would later become known as 'the Falstaff problem' can be illustrated by Barry Sullivan's 1797 *2 Henry IV*, which omitted Falstaff's rejection altogether to close with Henry IV's death in the Jerusalem chamber. At the King's death, all exclaimed, 'The King is dead! Long live the King!' three times and, as Henry IV's courtiers encircled the dead king's body, Hal knelt by his side to complete the tableau, which was accompanied by swelling organ music and a slow curtain fall.

Intriguingly enough, although these productions offer evidence of stretching the play to accommodate Falstaff and to serve as vehicles for major actors to play his role, the textual changes tend to marginalise his role – or at least to make Hal even more prominent. In addition, there were further indications of a commitment to staging 'real' history. Certainly the apotheosis of that occurred in an 1821 Covent Garden performance where, to commemorate the accession of George IV, *2 Henry IV* concluded with a spectacular coronation procession. Not only was the scene swollen with 'Princes, Peeresses, Judges, Bishops, Knights, Heralds, Pursuivants, Choristers' and others, but the pageant, praised by one reviewer for its 'liberality', was divided into four discrete scenes, one of which dramatised 'the entrée of the Challenger'. Londoners could even purchase a printed play-book which listed the order of procession and described the production's 'big' effects (Odell, II, pp. 166-9). In appropriating *2 Henry IV*'s ending to intersect with a particular moment in cultural history and turn it into a commercial theatrical success, Covent Garden's state occasion seems designed to overwhelm Falstaff with royal authority. Although none attempted such a lavish finale, later nineteenth-century productions also suggest that Falstaff's fortunes were waning. Hackett's 1841 production, for example, rid the commonwealth of Falstaff *before* the accession scene (V.ii), which closed the play. By omitting all references to Henry's relationship with his brothers ('I'll be your father and your brother too' [V.ii.57]) or with the Lord Chief Justice ('You shall be as a father to my youth' [V.ii.117]), Hackett's representational politics focused exclusively on Henry V's virtuous royal image: at the last, anticipating his coronation, he proclaims England an ideal state. By this time, it would seem, *2 Henry IV* not only had a highly institutionalised close but was fast becoming a royal history, not a Falstaff play.

A Falstaff play was, however, still being staged. By the mid- to late nineteenth century, *Merry Wives*, not the *Henrys*, was in fashion, a popularity that can be explained in terms of the growth of bourgeois sensibility. In 1874, however, Samuel Phelps cobbled together scenes from the *Henrys* as a preface for *Henry V*: he played

[10]

Falstaff in *Part One*, doubled Henry IV and Shallow in *Part Two* and then emerged as Henry V. What seemed to be on offer in this historical bricolage was Phelps's ability to take on so many guises; at the height of bourgeois individualism, the great actor became the theatrical equivalent of history's 'great man'. It was also the age of star roles, and although *2 Henry IV* was not a standard repertory play, Frank Benson did include it, together with *King John*, *Richard II*, *Henry V*, *2 Henry VI* and *Richard III* – all of which offer opportunities for strong individual performers – in his 1901 'Week of Kings' for Stratford's Shakespeare Memorial Theatre. Benson repeated that selection of plays in 1905–06: on both occasions, all the plays were heavily cut, some scenes were transposed, and they were not played as a sequence or in chronological order (Sprague, *Shakespeare's Histories*, p. 7). Nevertheless, if 'cycle' is taken to mean presenting a *series* of plays, Benson's can be considered the ancestor of later twentieth-century history cycles.

At least in England. For in 1864, to celebrate the tercentenary of Shakespeare's birth, Franz Dingelstedt had produced seven of Shakespeare's histories in Weimar, played in successive sequence over a week's time. And in 1935, the Pasadena, California Community Playhouse staged all ten history plays in succession, with one production closing before the next opened. Such an arrangement comes close to reproducing how late sixteenth-century spectators would have experienced the plays, and it persists in American Shakespeare repertory companies, such as Ashland's Oregon Shakespeare Festival, where a 'cycle' takes years to complete. But, although early twentieth-century British productions had linked *1* and *2 Henry IV*, the crucial moment of cycle production occurred in 1951, when Anthony Quayle and Michael Redgrave staged the *Henrys*, together with *Richard II* and *Henry V*, for their Festival of Britain season at Stratford's Shakespeare Memorial Theatre. And from this point forward, *2 Henry IV* has been performed most regularly as part of a larger 'epic' or 'grand design'. Perhaps the most important implication of that grand design is that it firmly re-situates *2 Henry IV* as a 'history play' in which Hal, not Falstaff, and the royal narrative, not the comic–popular history, are the main events. The evolution of that grand design and its institutionalisation as a theatrical construct also has its own history, which is closely bound up with shifting fashions about, and anxiety over, reproducing Shakespeare's 'intentions'. While the critics who reviewed the 1951 Quayle–Redgrave Festival productions eagerly accepted the notion that Shakespeare intended to (and did) write a great national epic, many who commented on the English Shakespeare Company's 1988–89 history sequence could argue just as authoritatively that Shakespeare never intended the plays for cycle production. Although these competing claims have to do in part with whether or not a critic did or did not approve of the ideologies driving both productions, what they also reveal is the historically specific relationship between literary and theatrical fashions.

This interdependency of literary and theatrical cultures tends to be overlooked, if not suppressed. The debate between those who prefer to read Shakespeare and those who prefer to experience his plays in the theatre has a long history that needs no rehearsal here, especially in a book whose readers are likely to be among those already 'receptive to the ever-varying discoveries theatrical interpretation provides' (Series Editors' preface). Reading and theatregoing are indeed experiences different in kind, but the notion that they remain entirely separate and distinct is shot through with contradictions. These are most obviously illustrated by the first and last productions described in this volume. At one end of the spectrum, Redgrave's 1951 Festival of Britain production boasted of its connections to literary culture, which came from E. M. W. Tillyard's reading of Shakespeare's histories as mirrors of Elizabethan policy. And at the other, the English Shakespeare Company's co-founder, Michael Bogdanov, claimed in 1986 that he wished to recover a Shakespeare obscured by academic notions and return him to his 'proper' place in theatrical culture. That claim needs to be taken with a grain of salt, however, for not only was Bogdanov's production attuned to recent currents in literary scholarship, but he was, like Quayle and Redgrave, reading the histories through the ideological imperatives specific to his particular historical and cultural moment. Indeed, it seems entirely appropriate to argue that few if any spectators, especially in the late twentieth century, come to the theatre with innocent eyes. In First-World countries – and, not incidentally, in those Third-World countries once under Britain's imperial rule – Shakespeare's plays have been put to use as an educational yardstick, required by secondary-school curricula and 'strongly recommended' as one mark of the so-called educated or civilised person. Not only, then, are directors, designers and actors likely to have read Shakespeare through the pervasive apparatus of academic culture, but spectators, including the woman on the street, the press reviewer and the academic critic, come to the theatre with general if not specific notions of what 'Shakespeare' is or *ought* to be. Although it will necessarily oversimplify these issues, a brief survey can suggest the extent to which critical discourse has both energised and responded to the changing cultural currents of theatrical interpretation.

Mid-eighteenth-century readers of *2 Henry IV* were most interested in explaining Falstaff, whom they theorised as a 'humours' character. What commentators found most appealing was his wit, and they were all too willing to forgive his cowardice and to take pleasure in him as a source of 'sport and diversion' (Morris, p. 3). Even Samuel Johnson, for whom Shakespeare's art was a moral enterprise, spends only enough time describing Prince Hal to prove that Shakespeare knew how to create a royal hero that is 'great, original and just'; the rest of his commentary praises Falstaff. But although Johnson obviously relished the fat knight, he was quick to conclude that 'no man is more dangerous than he that, with a will to corrupt, hath the power to please; and that neither wit nor honesty ought to think themselves safe with such a companion when they see Henry seduced by Falstaff' (p. 8). If, however, the corrupt misleader of youth could not be embraced wholeheartedly, Shakespeare himself could. And from this time forward, admiration for Falstaff went hand in hand with admiration for Shakespeare's artistry and 'genius'. William Hazlitt, writing in an age which romanticised individual subjectivity and was obsessed with character, memorialised Falstaff's magnificent self-sufficiency. His famous 1817 essay calls him 'the most substantial comic character that ever was invented'; and he concludes:

> The truth is that we never could forgive the Prince's treatment of Falstaff; though perhaps Shakespeare knew what was best, according to the history, the nature of the times, and of the man. We speak only as dramatic critics. Whatever terror the French in those days might have of Henry V, yet, to the readers of poetry at present, Falstaff is the better man of the two. We think of him and quote him oftener. (pp. 63-4)

There is perhaps no more persuasive evidence of a character's ability to exist outside a play, poem or novel than to 'own' him (in this case) through quotation – a function of education. Such attachment to Falstaff is a perennial theme. In 1902, A. C. Bradley, taking the rejection as the high-point of Shakespeare's deliberate degradation of the character, asked, 'What do we feel, and what are we meant to feel, as we witness this rejection? And what does our feeling imply as to the characters of Falstaff and the new King?' (p. 78). Like Hazlitt, Bradley's answers place him in Falstaff's camp, together with Shakespeare's 'genius'. But even the syntax of his questions points to the contradictions he attempts to negotiate – the difference between what we feel and what we are *meant* to feel and how such feelings impinge on the *characters* of Falstaff and Henry V, whom Bradley, like others before and after him, views as interdependent, the one taking meaning from the other.

Bradley's meticulous reading of Falstaff, Hal and the rejection has an elegaic tone: it might be Falstaff's epitaph, a farewell to sentiment and, for the moment, to characterology. For from this point forward, reading strategies explain Falstaff in terms of an overall *historical* design and by connecting him almost exclusively with his *theatrical* ancestors: the *miles gloriosus*, the Vice of the morality play and the Lord of Misrule, a figure later critics would theorise more fully through Saturnalian folk rituals and Carnival (see Wilson, Tillyard, Barber, Bristol). In part, this critical move had already been anticipated in the Victorian and Edwardian theatre, where 'historically accurate' pictorial stagings fed a widespread public interest in the distant past, energised in part by recent archaeological discoveries (see Booth, Meisel). But it was also a sign of renewed interest in recuperating an Elizabethan understanding of Shakespeare's play; and this particular archaeological retrieval was deeply implicated in the ideological prerogatives of mid-twentieth-century culture. When, in 1943, John Dover Wilson wrote that 'the technical centre of [the *Henrys*] is not the fat knight but the lean prince' (p. 117), he was not only privileging the plays' royal–historical narrative but refiguring *2 Henry IV* as a conversion story in which Shakespeare deliberately kept Hal from Falstaff in order to preserve respect for his princely character, the somewhat anxious explanation of a critic who assumes that the 'disease' which Falstaff is thought to figure is catching. His voice was joined by others, the most important being E. M. W. Tillyard, whose notion of the histories as Shakespeare's English epic, built around the theme of 'Respublica' and detailing 'the very nature of England', positioned *2 Henry IV* as a play in which Henry IV's death and Hal's appearance as Henry V become the 'true' (or 'historical') climaxes of an action centred on the education of the Prince, where Falstaff's rejection is seen as a moral (as well as dramatic) necessity to ensure an ordered and orderly state (Tillyard, p. 298). Accounting for 'the very nature of England' had significant historical import in 1944, as the Second World War was ending; and by finding a pattern of order in Shakespeare's history, Tillyard's best-selling study not only celebrated England's greatest literary figure but offered a model for reconstituting a post-war culture in which 'Shakespeare-history' could legitimate and validate the national self, the 'character' of England.

Ever since the Quayle–Redgrave 1951 Festival cycle, which translated Tillyard to the theatre, the matter of representing 'Elizabethan England' and English-history-as-the-Elizabethans-understood-it according to Tillyard has figured in some way in productions of *2 Henry IV*. Even when a production such as the English Shakespeare Company's counters Tillyard's ideas, his presence reappears, much like Hamlet's father's ghost or, perhaps more aptly, as Rumour, in reviewers' comments as the not-so-invisible standard which measures the 'appropriate' limits of later productions and, most especially, the limitations of Falstaff. The appeal of Tillyard's monolithic fiction is tied to a myth of ownership: the plays, so that myth goes, anatomise the nation; they belong to England. And in such a myth, while Hal and Henry IV *are* history, Falstaff *serves* it. That interdependent relationship between Hal and Falstaff, between a 'real' historical figure and an imagined one, perpetuates some of the double historical sensibility which scholars imagine to have been a component of late sixteenth-century spectators' experience of historical drama; it also reproduces some sense of the negotiation between literary and theatrical cultures, between written history and comic–popular dramatic traditions, which shape the plays.

While mid-century productions such as Redgrave's were at-tempting to give the 'Tudor myth' a full theatrical reality, literary critics were responding to or diverging from Tillyardism with a wide range of arguments framed, at first, by the New Criticism, and then by various strands of structuralist and post-structuralist theory. Although it would risk falsifying both critical and theatrical history to suggest a neat, linear movement from one interpretive strategy to another, it would be fair to say that each successive account of the *Henrys* had to encounter Tillyard, and it would also be fair to say that, in the second half of the twentieth century, theatrical practice became more selective in appropriating schol-arly interpretations. Perhaps the most widely influential critical practice was the concept of 'close reading' drawn from New Criti-cism. Royal Shakespeare Company directors such as John Barton and Trevor Nunn, whose university education under the tutelage of F. R. Leavis had trained them as close readers, brought those strategies for exploring Shakespeare's language to the rehearsal room; Terry Hands and Michael Bogdanov (also university-trained) inherited that practice, which not only resulted in new standards for verse-speaking but in attention to particular themes – disease, weariness, death and decay, all of which have, in various ways, been translated into individual productions' *mises-en-scène*. Psychoanalysis, that strand of academic discourse which has moved most easily into the popular culture of a post-Freudian age, offers a way of negotiating between the plays and spectators' every-day lived experience: the Oedipal conflict the *Henrys* dramatise is everyone's family drama, and productions by Terry Hands (1975), Trevor Nunn (1982) and Michael Bogdanov (1986-89) all empha-sise father–son relations, both in terms of their structural design and in the playing of individual moments. In addition, Stanislavskian, post-Stanislavskian and Method approaches to act-ing have prompted renewed attention to psychological characterology; even more specifically, insights into role-playing by psychologists such as Erving Goffman informed Terry Hands's *Henrys* in particular.

More specialised critical configurations of the plays have of-fered important correctives to Tillyard's somewhat rigid insistence on order as the underlying ideological principle driving Eliza-bethan culture. Combining insights from psychoanalysis and an-thropology, C. L. Barber's influential *Shakespeare's Festive Comedy* explores the similarities and differences between comedy and folk rituals; he viewed *2 Henry IV* as dramatising the trial of Carnival and read Falstaff's rejection as analogous to a scapegoating ritual in which the magic of kingship attempts to limit the unruly im-pulses set loose by Falstaff, managing the anxieties he represents (see pp. 213-21). Called by another name, the magic of kingship informs the work of recent new historicist critics, who focus on how the plays dramatise power relations – especially on how power consistently reconstitutes itself by containing disorder – and on examining the relationships between Elizabethan theatrical culture and other social practices (see especially Greenblatt). Informed by recent revisions of Marxist thought, cultural materialist and feminist critics recover a somewhat different 'new history', which reveals a subversive 'political Shakespeare' lurking beneath the conservative, protectionist ideology Tillyard attributed to him: while the plays absorb and refract late Elizabethan cultural prerogatives, they also contain a radical critique of the power relations shaping class and gender hierarchies (see especially Dollimore and Sinfield). Although the English Shakespeare Company's production found support for its analysis of political power in Dollimore and Sinfield's reading of *Henry V*, cultural materialist, new historicist, and feminist critical designs have not as yet become, like Tillyard's, institutionalised within theatrical practice. Instead, to borrow Raymond Williams's term, they contribute to an increasingly viable oppositional formation (pp. 118-19).

As such, they point to the vulnerability of Tillyard's myth of ownership or incorporation as a monolithic tradition of the surviving past. Where in 1951, staging Tillyard's intentionally selective version of Shakespeare-history as a model of order could serve to allay mid-century anxieties about Britain's social and cultural identification, redefinition, and renewal, late twentieth-century productions have made equally time-bound, equally selective negotiations between the shape of an Elizabethan past and the present. No one production fits any prescribed mould, nor can one assume that the Tillyardian era of production gives way to an era that is any less insistent on royalist prerogatives. In the theatre, as in other social and cultural endeavours, evolution is not a straightforward process; instead, it occurs in abrupt, jagged twists and turns that resist schematic constructs. Nevertheless, one constant joins the productions discussed in this volume. Each revival of the *Henrys* has marked a particular moment when, for sociopolitical and economic reasons, theatrical culture has seemed to be in jeopardy. In so far as such liminal circumstances have a Falstaffian ring, Falstaff would seem to be the most organic indicator of the character of the culture: though always rejected, his figure remains ready to turn 'history' into a theatrical commodity. Tracing how a Falstaff accommodates to or, to use Bardolph's phrase, is accommodated with, a production is crucial to the history of how *2 Henry IV* has been appropriated to serve various visions of 'England', whether by offering up the illusion of direct access to the Elizabethan age, by attempting to reproduce 'Shakespearian' staging (or both), or by giving voice to some match between the contradictory shape of Shakespeare-history and that of a present-day historical moment. As Rumour suggests, the historical fictions a nation, or perhaps more accurately, a nation's theatre, constructs are among the most persuasive it has.

[17]

CHAPTER II

'This wonderful chronicle': Michael Redgrave (1951)

I

Michael Redgrave's 1951 production of *2 Henry IV* dates from the third season of Anthony Quayle's directorship of the Shakespeare Memorial Theatre: a year which marked an extraordinary, even revolutionary moment of collaboration between theatrical and literary communities. As its contribution to the Festival of Britain, and for the first time in *British* theatrical history, the Stratford Summer Festival staged *Richard II*, *1* and *2 Henry IV* and *Henry V* together as a unified whole. Quayle's bold idea of mounting a sequence of English histories perfectly conjoined the best-selling studies of E. M. W. Tillyard and Lily B. Campbell, which constructed an Elizabethan World Picture as the ordering principle driving Shakespeare's historical project, and the Festival's theme, 'The Autobiography of a Nation', as well as its aim: to demonstrate post-war Britain's 'moral, cultural, spiritual and material' recovery and reconstruction. In retrospect, this cultural alliance between the Festival's desire to tell 'the island story' and Shakespeare's dramatisation of three reigns can be seen as an attempt to mobilise what Graham Holderness has called the Shakespeare myth to serve a distinctly nationalistic cause, committed more to reifying Britain's glorious past than to initiating progressive change (*Shakespeare's History*, pp. 203-6). But what may now appear politically conservative, even reactionary, was at the time a radical break with *theatrical* tradition, an unprecedented occasion where literary scholarship not only took to but actually spoke on the stage.

When Quayle became artistic director of the Stratford Festival in 1948, his predecessor, Sir Barry Jackson, urged him to foster relations between the Memorial Theatre and Shakespearian scholars, advice to which Quayle responded that 'as far as he was concerned the academics were the ivy on the tree, and it was the tree that needed to flourish' (Beauman 1982, p. 194). Yet what Quayle apparently viewed initially as a parasitic relationship he later represented, in his foreword to a commemorative record of the Festival productions, as a symbiotic binding together of 'the functions of three professions – those of actor, scholar and critic – all of them essential to the theatre' (Wilson and Worsley, p. vi). And, although scholarly and critical voices predominate in the volume, selective quotation gives theatrical artists what Quayle claims they desire: 'to have their performances purchased for the nation and fill a space or two in the Tate Gallery, or endure for posterity in a uniform edition, handsomely bound, the copyright jealously guarded by a fashionable publishing house' (Wilson and Worsley, p. ix). Turning first to that memorial document opens a window on to the literary–theatrical contexts and interpretive politics which shaped Redgrave's staging of the tetralogy and, more especially, his *2 Henry IV*, its 'third act', in which Quayle himself appeared as Falstaff.

Once bound together by tetralogy thinking, which assumed an inner unity and dramatic progression *intended* by Shakespeare and re-authorised by Tillyard's and Campbell's readings, the four plays emerged, in Dover Wilson's view, as an early modern analogue to Hardy's *Dynasts*. Citing the Folio organisation of the plays, which separates 'histories' from 'comedies' and 'tragedies', Wilson could easily justify Shakespeare's particular connection to British history and so claim 'the Master' as the realm's historiographical genius (p. 4). Furthermore, the Quayle–Redgrave project had the effect of erasing nineteenth- and early twentieth-century stagings, supplanting them with an interpretive vision 'true' to history as well as to Shakespeare. 'No one who witnessed with a proper understanding', wrote Wilson, 'will ever again be able to think of Falstaff and his royal partner, whether as Prince Hal or King Henry V, in the way Hazlitt and Swinburne, Bradley and Masefield, had taught us to think of them.' Such a 'proper understanding' also meant giving up universalist configurations of the plays and, instead, appraising the characters in terms of the political issues current in their historical moment. Then, and only then, might present-day spectators supposedly see with Elizabethan eyes and comprehend that 'both dramatist and audience are less concerned with the career and fortunes of the principal characters than with 'the sanity and health of this whole state' of England' (pp. 5-6).

Whether or not these particular dynamics of reception applied to the 1590s – and, with an ageing spinster on the throne and no heir named, they may well have – Wilson's statement almost certainly expressed the concerns of those spectators in 1951 whose desire for post-war social stability might find comforting echoes in Tillyard and Campbell's newly theorised Tudor rage for order. Certainly, too, the history forecast by the newly tetralogised plays bettered that which Britain would actually face in the 1950s: the loss of India had severely eroded remaining vestiges of colonial power, turning 'Empire' to 'Commonwealth', and slumps in the post-war European economy had brought severe economic crises (see Briggs, pp. 274-94). Amid gloomy forecasts of cultural decline, what could be more appropriate than to recirculate, retell, and re-theorise Britain's historical past? Even the numbers telling the decades seem remarkably complicit with making plays written in the 1590s speak to the 1950s: in our end is our beginning.

If Shakespeare's plays had been reclaimed for literary history, it also became necessary to rethink their past theatrical interpretation. Certainly a view of the plays as dramatising an overarching historical plan had several distinct theatrical advantages. According to Quayle, cycle presentation made it possible for a production to clarify, and capitalise upon, the literary as well as dramatic echoes among all four; not only did characters' lives begin to assume developmental patterns, but what had seemed to be puzzling psychological inconsistencies between the plays were now revealed as purposeful and masterful writing (Wilson and Worsley, p. vii). Moreover, 'too persuasive and dominant performances of parts which the author intended to be by no means so sympathetic', wrote Quayle, had marred Shakespeare's epic design (Wilson and Worsley, p. viii). The contemporary practice of presenting the plays exclusively as star vehicles had led to *Richard II*s in which Bolingbroke, and indeed the entire political narrative, became secondary to Richard's personal tragedy; *Henry V*, long regarded as a patriotic drum-and-trumpet pageant, was performed primarily to display the verbal skills of actors who could, as Clement McCallin was advised when he played Henry at Stratford in 1937, 'make the bells ring with the speeches, like Lewis Waller' (Beauman 1982, p. 206). The *Henry IV* plays were not, of course, exempt from either the perceived 'psychological inconsistencies' – attributed to the texts as well as to their previous theatrical adaptations – or from the 'distortions' of what were now considered to be false interpretations. And this was especially true of *2 Henry IV* – in Richard David's phrase, 'that ramshackle rag-bag of a piece' filled with Falstaffian 'sideshows' (*Shakespeare Survey*, p. 137). Wrote Quayle:

> Falstaff himself is a tremendous star-vehicle, and few stars will risk their chances of success by showing the unsympathetic, even repellent side of his character: how can they when the commercial success of Part II (presented singly) must depend on Falstaff's popularity? ... Finally, there is Hal – usually so shorn and mangled in both parts of *Henry IV* that he is unrecognizable when he emerges into *Henry V*, and so misrepresented as the frank, boon companion of Falstaff that we can only feel nauseated by his priggish renunciation of his friend. (Wilson and Worsley, p. viii)

In identifying those features of the play most resistant to what was to be a 'searching study of kingship', Quayle hints at the tension between commercialism (Falstaff) and history (Hal), condensed in terms of the play's most striking scene. Given the cycle's thrust towards generating Henry V (in Redgrave's programme note, the epic's 'true hero'), Falstaff – especially the Falstaff of *Part Two*, and most especially the sentimentalised Falstaff of the rejection scene – becomes a somewhat embarrassing, even disruptive, star presence. If the productions were indeed to dispel the 'mountain of misrepresentation and fog of ignorance built up over centuries of theatrical interpretation' and so to 'rediscover and try to reveal the author's true intentions' (Wilson and Worsley, p. ix), it was, in Quayle's view, crucial not only to recruit a uniformly strong acting company but to set a course that would refashion Hal, particularly in his relationship to Falstaff, and to turn Falstaffian diseases to an historical commodity.

In spite of his belief that the star system had contributed to blurring Shakespeare's theatrical design, Quayle's desire to transform the Memorial into the foremost classical theatre in the country, and so to rival London's Old Vic, clearly required luring star performers away from more commercial (and more profitable) West End venues to provincial Stratford. At a time when the idea of an ensemble company devoted to exploring Shakespeare was still foreign to English theatre, and when the critical community still assumed that a star system was in place, the dual commitment to theatrical excellence and commercial prestige could be achieved only by reproducing H. M. Tennent's tried and true managerial formula: gathering the best possible company – directors, designers, supporting actors and walk-ons – around a constellation of leading performers (Beauman 1982, pp. 199-200). With two successful Stratford seasons behind him and the tetralogy as a draw, Quayle was able to enlist Harry Andrews, who had spent two years at Stratford, for the role of Bolingbroke, and Michael Redgrave, who would play Richard II and Hotspur and direct *2 Henry IV*. Further choices supplied the most necessary correctives to that play's Falstaffian problems. Since the overall conception was Quayle's, and since he played Falstaff, he was responsible for downplaying sentimentality and so making the character conform to the requirements of the Festival design. Casting Richard Burton, whose 'star quality' was on the rise, as Prince Hal was the other ingredient in the new equation. Considered a risky choice in that some doubted his ability to rise to the role as well as to its rhetorical requirements – doubts remarkably congruent with Henry IV's opinion of his son – Burton brought an inner reserve and 'far-away Welsh look' to his reconception of Hal, a far cry from 'the customary cheerful wild-oat sowing'. Here, according to T. C. Worsley, was a Prince who laughed not with Falstaff but at him, whose looks masked his thoughts, and whose eyes, from the start, always seemed focused on his future destiny (Wilson and Worsley, pp. 32-3; 51-2).

Once again, too, literary scholarship shored up 'authorial intention' and theatrical rediscovery. By claiming the *Henry IV* plays as Shakespeare's great Tudor morality, the consummation of a long tradition of prodigal-son dramas, and by figuring Falstaff as Vice, Devil and Lord of Misrule in a saga designed to produce, and then uphold, right royalty, Dover Wilson further justified re-reading the Hal–Falstaff dynamic. It was important, he thought, to see the plays with Elizabethan eyes. Just as their fathers did not question the necessity of the Vice being carried to Hell in the old plays, Shakespeare's audiences would neither question nor deplore Falstaff's downfall and arrest. Moreover, those famous latter-day critics (Bradley among them) who judged Henry V so harshly for rejecting Falstaff would find themselves outnumbered among Wilson's conjectural late Elizabethan spectators, who would never think of questioning the monarch or, even more significantly, the Rule of Law, in the person of the Lord Chief Justice, which stands behind him (pp. 23-30). In order to re-educate Festival spectators to this early modern vision of the order of things, Redgrave's programme note for *2 Henry IV* contains rather explicit interpretive instructions:

> [Henry V's] so-called 'rejection' of Falstaff may to some extent disappoint our sympathies, but from the beginning he has prepared us and even Falstaff for nothing else but this. The fact that he repudiates him publicly is forced on him by Falstaff, and the conditions he imposes, which include a competence for life, can scarcely be called severe. The rebuke, we are told later, kills Falstaff's heart, and, loving Falstaff, we cannot but grieve for it. But in terms of kingship the rebuke is necessary and, in the light of the play which is still to come, the alternative is unthinkable.

With remarkably accommodating eyes, the cycle's reviewers endorsed the newly tetralogised *2 Henry IV* and were enthusiastic about what the plays gained from chronicle presentation. The *Daily Telegraph*'s critic called it 'a piece of significant history' in which, according to Worsley, a 'superbly funny but openly contemptible' Falstaff no longer occupies an intractable position but is 'brought into a proper proportion'. It was history and drama, not fooling, that the critics who speak in the memorial volume remembered and praised: they singled out Henry IV's death as the play's climax and viewed the rejection as a necessary step in 'Prince Hal's apprenticeship to Royalty, ... indeed the sacrifice which we see Royalty exacting relentlessly from those worthy to assume it' (Wilson and Worsley, pp. 68, 72-3, 78). Paying a sentimental tribute to the links between Shakespeare's 'genius' and that of the producers, Robert Speaight attributed the cycle's success to a 'true originality' which lay in 'discovering what Shakespeare meant and in faithfully recording it'. To present the four histories as a single drama required 'look[ing] at Shakespeare straight', and at Falstaff in particular:

> It is one consequence of treating the plays in this way that the problem of Falstaff disappears, or rather the audience's problem is the same as Shakespeare's – how best to get rid of him. His comic stature is in no way reduced, but we see him for what he is – a gigantic excrescence on the surface of the plays, the sign of Shakespeare's creative genius, the symbol of a genial and quite intolerable anarchy .... By the time 'Harry has succeeded Harry' we have had enough of him. He and his companions have served their dramatic purpose which was to show us the 'other England' of slum and shire – the England that Henry was to govern and which, in order to govern, he had in some measure to know.

Concluding his praise of the Festival presentation, Speaight speaks, much like Falstaff advertising the virtues of sherris-sack, of 'rich rewards for the playgoer, new light for the student, and ripe instruction for anyone concerned with the management of the common weal' (Wilson and Worsley, pp. 88-90). Though Quayle's initial plan may have sought to banish notions of theatrical stardom, he had, much like Henry IV, only effected an exchange. Basing its legitimacy on a rare congruence of scholarly, theatrical, and critical authorities, the Festival cycle marked a watershed moment in which theatrical representation positioned *2 Henry IV* as part of a mid-century *Mirror for Magistrates* and planted Henry V as 'this star of England' – a figure capable of managing the cultural tensions of post-war Britain.

II

When Quayle was appointed as artistic director of the Shakespeare Memorial Theatre, he inherited an institution caught in circumstances somewhat analogous to those plaguing Henry IV's 'troublesome reign'. The dangers, however, came not so much from rebellions within the theatrical realm (though there were those who opposed Quayle's appointment as well as his plan to stage the histories) as from low cash reserves and gloomy financial prospects, exacerbated by a history of failures to capitalise the theatre's investment in landholdings. As Quayle himself put it, throughout the 1950s the Memorial Theatre 'led a knife-edge existence financially' (Beauman 1982, p. 201). To add to these curiously Falstaffian problems, the theatre building itself had fallen into disrepair. Long considered a nearly impossible playing space – George Devine had called it 'that great lump of masonry' and had suggested sinking it and starting over – the Memorial was, during the winter before the Festival of Britain year, 'patched up for heaven'. As Sally Beauman reports, 'the circle was cantilevered forward, with side additions curving towards the stage, the stalls were re-stepped to improve sight-lines, and the proscenium arch was restyled; the forestage was enlarged, and the entire auditorium redecorated and reseated. New lighting and sound equipment was installed, and a new wing of dressing-rooms was built' (p. 205).

At a cost of £100,000, this new theatrical 'body' substantially reduced any reserve capital, but the gains – a more intimate connection between player and spectator – brought the Memorial closer to approximating the Elizabethan ideals embodied in the open-stage movement currently in vogue (see Styan, pp. 180-205). Indeed these physical changes were forerunners of others made in the 1960s when, under Peter Hall's direction, the Stratford Festival became the Royal Shakespeare Company and the interest in recuperating methods of Elizabethan staging reached its peak.

So renovated, the stage could better accommodate Tanya Moiseiwitsch's permanent set design, a radically innovative departure from the opulently 'accurate' historical realism of late nineteenth- and early twentieth-century 'realisations' (see Meisel; Booth) and an element crucial to the histories' unified presentation. Although the Memorial stage space did not fully escape the constrictions of illusionistic realism deriving from the proscenium arch, Moiseiwitsch's set, modelled on the Elizabethan public stage, not only simulated (and celebrated) the plays' original theatrical circumstances but enhanced the aura of archaeological recovery surrounding the Quayle–Redgrave project. Designed to offer three flexible playing spaces and a large variety of entrances and exits, the set was a scaffold-like structure, with stairs curving down either side and topped by a gallery or space 'aloft', framed by smoky blue draperies. This central façade was flanked at stage left by a penthouse and at right, near the proscenium wall, by the 'royalty corner', the site of the throne, which remained on stage throughout; on the curtainless stage, it was often the first area picked out as the lights came up at the beginning of each of the production's acts. The space beneath the bridge could be closed off by massive doors; when open, the upstage area behind it might function as an inner stage or evoke the public reaches of street and forest. Positioned at mid-stage in order to provide the largest possible downstage playing platform, Moiseiwitsch's set permitted the action to unfold swiftly and without interruption across it, a feature praised by most reviewers, though one, noting that the programme identified the scene as 'England', remarked :

> Our foreign visitors will carry away a curious impression of this country in the fifteenth century if they believe that the Archbishop's palace at York, Justice Shallow's house in Gloucestershire, Northumberland's castle at Warkworth, the Boar's Head Tavern at Eastcheap, the Palace of Westminster, Gaultree Forest in Yorkshire, and various streets in London all conformed to a standardised pattern of planks, poles and platforms. (*Nottingham Guardian*, 10 May 1951)

But however much the pseudo-Elizabethan stage 'house' prompted longings for former picturesque theatrical traditions, the richly detailed period costumes, also designed by Moiseiwitsch, supplied that lack. They not only 'sat on their wearers with an every-day comfortableness and seemed inevitable' – a virtue that strengthened the production's commitment to historicity (David, *Shakespeare Survey*, pp. 130-1) – but contributed, again as in the Elizabethan theatre, to privileging actors' presences and to making especially noticeable those moments of performance (particularly for Hal and Falstaff) where a change of costume marks a change in role.

Michael Redgrave's preparation copy maps the production's staging with a precision demanded by common theatrical practice, when four weeks' rehearsal time necessitated and tradition dictated a producer's fairly strict control. In this document, Redgrave not only localises each scene carefully, either by means of a particular property, such as a wattle garden seat and bench for Shallow's orchard, or an explanatory dumb-show (at times serving to dress the stage or to remove its furniture), but plots a physical configuration for each. Throughout, he pays particular attention to patterning a variety of entrances and exits, reserving the use of the huge up-centre doors to point especially significant ones. His notations for music also key the mood of a scene as well as register class difference: 'royal ta<u>ras</u>' to accompany the entrances of the King and nobles, plainsong to play through the Archbishop's plotting (I.iii) and 'sad, distressed music' for the King's death measure out an emphasis on rule that contrasts with the use of 'bizarre' tunes for the tavern–brothel, 'countryside gambols' for the recruiting and a 'rustic bumpkinry prelude of scherzo-like nature' to introduce the Gloucestershire revels. Intriguingly, the preparation copy cuts off with a single note – 'moonlight again' – in the last Gloucestershire scene (V.iii), suggesting that the play's final, inevitable moments require no preliminary outline. In fact very few deviations from Redgrave's original thinking occur in the prompt copy: reading both existing records together makes it possible not only to recuperate the production's textual and structural emphases and to visualise its staging but to speculate on how those strategies channelled this *2 Henry IV* towards a particular ideological configuration as well.

The text used was the New Temple edition, a series prepared in accord with scholarly principles but with a minimal apparatus, to which Redgrave's preparation copy only occasionally refers. Cuts are surprisingly judicious: the overall principle is to eliminate repetition (except in the case of Shallow, whose dramatic life depends upon it) and quicken narrative drive, retaining only what is necessary to establish a point or to permit an actor's thought to travel from one idea to the next – strategies that anticipate John Barton's in his more heavily reworked 1964 adaptations of the *Henry VI* plays and *Richard III* (see Barton and Hall). Redgrave deletes material that recalls events in *Richard II* and *1 Henry IV* and is not essential to the scene at hand. In the Gaultree betrayal (IV.i; IV.ii), for example, cuts sharpen the scenes' dramatic and political energies by redirecting long set speeches towards more conversational rhythms; even Henry IV's lengthy deathbed speech (IV.v) loses sixteen reminiscent lines. Also gone are lines that describe an action or attitude which can instead be established physically; in addition, obscure classical allusions as well as topical references, such as Hal's superfluous comments on stockings and linen (II.ii) or those to Lent and meat-eating (II.iv), are stripped away, as are the most potentially offensive sexual innuendos of Fang, Snare and Mistress Quickly, including her 'call me madam' (II.i.101). Aside from the exceptions noted (and one to which I shall return), the royals and nobility get their script more or less intact – a move that emphasises *2 Henry IV* as hegemonic succession history. Most deletions rob the realm's subjects of their 'local' quirks of phrase, and, since rather heavy cuts shorten Falstaff's role as well (especially his soliloquy turns), the theatrical knight, in this as in later stagings, is a more streamlined man of words and wit than the speech-fattened figure readers encounter.

Redgrave shapes *2 Henry IV* into three acts, each climaxing in a striking scene or spectacle. Structurally, this choice divides the play into rather severely enclosed playlets which trace a hierarchical progression: the acts might be titled 'Falstaff', 'Henry IV', and 'Henry V' or, following Auden's imagined play, 'Symptoms of Disease', 'The Doctor Arrives', and 'Recovery'. Intervals follow the famous tavern–brothel scene (II.iv) and Henry IV's death (IV.v) – judging from the number of critics who mention it, a choice which enhanced its importance – and the play ends, of course, with the famous rejection. Each internal close, then, not only stresses Hal's growing distance from Falstaff – what Samuel Crowl, writing of Orson Welles's 1966 *Chimes at Midnight*, has called 'The Long Goodbye' – but invites correspondences with the earlier plays. The first brings Hal and Falstaff together to echo *Part One*'s tavern playlet (II.v); then, a reprise of *Part One*'s father–son interview cements Hal's title to the crown (IV.v); finally, in the coronation scene, Hal's turning away from Falstaff is followed by a processional exit which recalls *Richard II*'s closing moments and, beyond that, pays homage to earlier theatrical occasions when the royal entry was staged to approximate a 'real' coronation. If enforcing the connections, continuities, and likenesses among the plays welded them into what some critics considered an overly aggressive unity that worked against highlighting their differences, further evidence of that appears in Redgrave's initial notations for the music, which, he writes, should (1) establish a relation to *Part One*; (2) mark Henry IV's death and the end of his 'troublesome reign' with a 'sombre note' (one more sombre than that for Hotspur's death in *Part One*), and (3) 'strike a new note' for the coronation, 'presag[ing] the dominating sound for *Henry V*'. Intriguingly, Redgrave did reject one of his original ideas for orchestrating such connections. Because he thought that *Part Two* lacked the bustle of *Part One*'s battle scenes, his preparation copy suggests staging a 'particularly bloody engagement' between two captains just before Coleville enounters Falstaff at Gaultree – presumably to mark Gaultree's diminished chivalry, provide a realistic basis for Coleville's surrender, and, perhaps most importantly, echo Shrewsbury's Hal–Hotspur combat as well as its Falstaffian aftermath. But whether or not he eventually dropped the fight because it took up too much time or because it finally seemed unnecessary remains conjectural.

Whatever the case, Shrewsbury did recur in the production's startling opening, where faint thunder replaced the customary overture and where, as the lights came up, spectators saw a fiery cresset, smoke, and Northumberland's tattered battle flag blowing in the wind. Lanterns and torches pierced the darkened stage, a wounded man was brought in, and a drunken soldier entered, singing over the wind. As swords were drawn and a scuffle began, one of the figures held up a lantern to reveal Rumour's face – a ghastly white mask – and his fantastically coiffed hair; when he laughed, exposing a long, lolling red tongue, all on stage froze and, at a thunder-clap, he moved to the downstage steps to speak. Echoed offstage in disunison, his words were punctuated with trumpet fanfares and, at his mention of the 'crafty-sick' Northumberland, by tympani and a roll of drums, signalling the verbal rush of Shrewsbury rumours into the play's first scene. The wind died, the figures cleared the stage and, with the cresset of flames nearly extinguished, bolts were drawn back on the up-centre doors to admit the messengers. Hearing their reports, Northumberland stood locked in a trance of grief and guilt until, throwing away his crutch, he cried out his final lines.

By representing post-battle confusions as breeding rumours, this *2 Henry IV* reached back into theatrical history and to historical dramas such as *Gorboduc* (1562), in which explanatory dumb-shows opened each act, sketching out what was to come. But such an homage to Elizabethan recovery was perhaps less immediate than how Rumour's appearance presaged, first, Northumberland's sick white face and, more importantly, Falstaff's over-painted red and white make-up, grotesque nose, stand-out curly forelock and sideburns – signs of theatricality serving to link both figures to artifice and disguise. And, although the production's overall emphasis on telling 'real' history did not consistently exploit the possibilities of fictive role-playing, these connections were playfully extended when, even though 'old Double is dead', the actor playing Rumour (William Squire) reappeared as Silence.

Once the play reached Falstaff's encounter with the Lord Chief Justice, yet another mime transformed the stage space with signs reminiscent of 'Merrie England' – a myth popularised twenty years before in a number of richly detailed, 'authentically' historical films, among them Alexander Korda's 1933 *The Private Life of Henry VIII* and Michael Curtiz's 1939 *The Private Lives of Elizabeth and Essex*. Supers crossed the stage calling out 'Hot codlings, hot', 'hot sheeps' feet', 'rushes green' and 'wood to cleave'; some put up signs for the 'Lamplighter Inn'; a butcher opened his shop-front; a bird-seller entered on the bridge with cages of linnets, finches and starlings; thrown out of an alehouse, rough soldiers weaved across the stage singing as a housewife threw slops on them while 'spare children' played a game on the most prominent downstage steps. Theatricalising this particular vision of Elizabethan daily life has the effect of naturalising it and according it transhistorical continuity. Moreover, such iconic realism not only establishes 'England' as a realm of shopkeepers but figures a post-Shrewsbury realm of appetite where marginal men and base trades flourish side by side and so creates a pseudo-historical context for Falstaff. And indeed, a butcher's apprentice brought an enormous, greasy-looking carcass of English beef through the central doors at precisely the moment Falstaff entered, wearing an old but rather grand fur-trimmed long coat which hid his gouty foot; his page, well-dressed only in this scene, carried his Shrewsbury sword and buckler – 'proofs' of Falstaff's war record. A 'Bona Roba' (noted as such in both preparation and prompt copies) came out from the upstage-left brothel with a soldier, walked him to upstage centre and waved goodbye; spying her, Falstaff hobbled with some dignity to catch sight of her as she returned to the brothel; they exchanged looks, and Falstaff attempted to follow her in on 'thou art fitter to be worn in my cap than to wait at my heels' (I.ii.15-16). Noting the Lord Chief Justice, who entered from the bridge, crossing from right to left to descend to the platform, Falstaff attempted to hide in the archway surrounding the up-centre doors but only succeeded in drawing attention to himself. When the conversation turned to tallow and gravy, the Lord Chief Justice and Falstaff were directly in front of the butcher's shop; and lights dimmed on the up-left brothel as the Lord Chief Justice accused Falstaff of being old.

Encoding Falstaff by means of these social markers and stage moves accomplished more, however, than simply identifying him as the Vice-like Lord of Misrule. Just as Hal's 'I know you all' soliloquy and the close of the tavern playlet in *Part One* foretold the play's ending, Redgrave choreographed features of this scene, together with Mistress Quickly's accusations and the tavern scene which closes the act, to anticipate later blocking and, with it, the final rejection. The 'Bona Roba', as well as the emphasis on Falstaff's sexuality and his age signalled by the brothel's dimming lights would, of course, become linked textually once Doll Tearsheet appears; even more strikingly, two scenes later Hal would repeat the Lord Chief Justice's entrance, as would Henry IV in the second act opening; finally, that entrance would be paralleled yet again by Henry V's coronation procession, where once more Falstaff stood by the up-centre doors, this time waiting to greet 'royal Hal'. Although this first act placed Falstaff at the centre of a noisy, boisterously commercial spectacle, that spectacle not only served the production's 'historical' purposes but looked forward to his demise; and the 'royalty corner', with its as yet unused throne, charged the margins of the stage with an additional reminder of what waits in the wings.

Further anticipatory cues, achieved either by other instances of repetitive blocking or by pointing particular moments, traced through the following scenes and culminated in the tavern–brothel scene which closes the act. Bardolph, defending Falstaff in the scuffle with the law (II.i), pinned Fang to the ground, causing the Bona Roba to scream with laughter and kiss Bardolph; from the bridge, a woman threw wet washing at Snare. Tellingly, such popular distaste for the law comes from women, whose 'faults' and 'unruly' behaviours are rather conventionally coded. At the height of the brawl, Quickly raised her skirts as though afraid of a mouse, only to be embarrassed by the Lord Chief Justice's entrance; 'goodwife Keech, the butcher's wife' started to reply as Quickly mentioned her (II.i.95-6), but her husband slapped a hand over her mouth; and, in the act's final scene, much comic business arose from Quickly's imitating Pistol's swagger and from an extremely drunken Doll, who pursued Pistol with a fruit-knife. If these moments glance forward and seem to 'justify' the Doll-Quickly arrest (V.iv), that was even more specifically presaged when, as the Lord Chief Justice accused Falstaff of having 'practised upon the easy-yielding spirit of this woman' (II.i.116-17), Quickly mistook his civilised tone for kindness, burst into tears and sobbed on his shoulder, only to be turned away by his cold rebuke, 'Pray thee, peace' (II.i.120).

Almost uniformly, reviewers noted that the play gives short shrift to its women characters, observations that have their own history. Objecting to the lack of a prominent female character, early nineteenth-century 'lady audiences' did not favour 2 Henry IV, or the other Falstaff plays, with their patronage, an aversion Priestley explained as hostility to Falstaff but which has been more adequately theorised by recent critical explorations of Falstaff's 'feminine' traits, from his womb-like belly to his seemingly unbridled tongue (see Kahn, Traub, Hodgdon 1991). Earlier productions had attempted to correct this gender imbalance by casting women as Falstaff's page, occasionally as Gloucester and Clarence, and even as Rumour – according to A. C. Sprague, a gendering that 'seems more natural', especially if the actress doubles as Doll Tearsheet (p. 78; 78n; see also Berger). But such moves could not erase the vexed problem of the play's most 'dangerous' scene, the tavern–brothel – usually bowdlerised but often omitted because 'no principal actress will condescend to speak but two speeches'. The Bensons' late nineteenth-century Stratford productions had prompted especially vigorous responses from women spectators. Lady Benson writes of 'the enforced exit of groups of schoolgirls during the playing of the Tavern Scene and of receiving expostulating letters (she played Doll Tearsheet), one of which ended with the words, "I could never watch you again as 'Juliet', knowing to what depths you can sink'" (quoted in Sprague, pp. 75n; 74).

The exception to these perceived lapses in Shakespeare's moral taste, of course, is Lady Percy – also a woman rebel, though appropriately contained by her moving eulogy on the chivalrous Hotspur. In Redgrave's *2 Henry IV*, she wore his ring around her neck and, at her entrance, looked out the opening in the façade where, in *Part One*, Hotspur had called for his horse. Intriguingly, critical reactions to Barbara Jefford's performance – 'the most moving single episode in the whole series'; spoken 'with a sort of hushed intensity' (David, *Shakespeare Survey*, p. 132; Sprague, p. 83) – appeared a year or more following the production. First-night reviewers focused instead on Heather Stannard's Doll – 'a born trollop,' wrote the *Liverpool Post*'s knowing critic (9 May 1951) – who, according to the *Birmingham Post*, 'acts to excess in her anxiety to leave no vulgarity undemonstrated' (9 May 1951). Much in the spirit of the 1906 critic who marvelled that an actress could be found 'to represent such an abandoned creature' (Sprague, p. 76n), an *Evening Standard* reporter charged Quayle and Redgrave with miscasting the actress who, the season before, had been Olivier's leading lady in Christopher Fry's *Venus Observed* (12 May 1951). However necessary it might be to establish Falstaff within a milieu marked by depravity and sexual diseases – Redgrave's preparation copy notes Dover Wilson's suggestion that Falstaff enter singing at left and exit right to point his famous 'Empty the jordan' (II.iv.33) – such staging should not tarnish the reputation of a rising *ingénue*.

If, however, the production seemed to damage Stannard by casting her against type, it certainly enhanced Burton's star image. His first appearance as Hal, like his last as Henry V, centred on a change of costume. He entered accompanied by Poins, who carried his 'war suit' (presumably Shrewsbury's tabard and armour) and a servant, who placed his 'new' clothes – 'something gay and jeune premier', notes the preparation copy – in front of the throne. What the preparation copy marks as simply taking off a cloak became even more pointed when, on 'let the end try the man' (II.ii.40), Hal removed his dressing-gown; by the time Bardolph and the Page entered (the latter in a grimy suit and wearing the Bona Roba's feather: in this *2 Henry IV*, sexual traffic knows no age), he is newly attired. What followed reprised *Part One*'s Gadshill robbery (through a coin-flipping exchange), revealed Hal's kindness to the

Page, his mistrust of Poins (and his sister, as well as the 'Ephesians,' 'pagans' and 'kinswomen', demonising terms which the prompt copy underlines) and, in making Bardolph the loser at both verbal and courtesy games, looked ahead to his being 'cut off' as an offender in *Henry V* (III.vi). Later, when Peto brought the summons from Westminster, Hal moved from his sideline position of mocking voyeur to replace Falstaff as the center of a final tableau, with all the principals lined up on either side of his suddenly still figure.

While lecturers in Stratford spoke, during the opening weeks of the production, of the plays' relationship to history and Elizabethan political theory (see *Stratford-upon-Avon Herald*, 18 May 1951), critics focused on the production's visual style as well as its familiar Falstaffian humours:

> Mr Redgrave has softened [the set's] asperity by glimpses of lighted interiors and of side-booths and shops opened for London's traffic. It is a welcome touch and helps one to over- look too much stridency in the tavern scenes, though Rosalind Atkinson can still endow Mistress Quickly with a shrewish kick that seems not out of keeping. (*Manchester Guardian Weekly*, 17 May 1951)

> [Quayle's Falstaff] has a mischievous twinkle in his roving old eye, a wicked old smile playing over his round mouth, and the legs under the enormous paunch certainly look old in iniquity, though they are preternaturally active for their age. (*News Chronicle*, 9 May 1951)

Others, however, were alert to Quayle's reconception of the character as well as to the reasoning behind it:

> As Falstaff, Anthony Quayle develops the knight along the lines of rascality, hauteur, and artfulness which he laid down in Part 1 of the play, but the old man grows more vehement in villainy. Mr. Quayle makes no bones about the rascality. Falstaff's misdemeanours are no gentlemanly lapses, though they are excused in aristocratic accents. They are the deliberate doings of one who knows he has a bad name and is determined to live up to it. (*Birmingham Post*, 9 May 1951)

> Anthony Quayle's Falstaff ... loomed (or rather bloomed) almost larger than life. Too many actors we have, resting too heavily on the laurels of Sir John's immortality, presume on audiences as on the young prince with their slapstick. Mr. Quayle's performance had the restraint of a discerning artist, while lacking nothing in flesh and blood. (*Royal Leamington Spa Courier*, 11 July 1951)

> In the interests of the apologia [for history] Mr. Anthony Quayle deliberately presents a Falstaff who is scarcely likeable. We cannot but admire the wit which has survived physical and moral degeneration, but we observe that he uses it merely to get himself out of scrapes. He has little

pleasure in it for its own sake: there is always a shifty and calculating look in his eye, and he is never certain of his hold on the prince. No wonder, for even in the comparatively carefree days of the Gadshill robbery, as we remember, the prince of Mr. Richard Burton was a detached and rather critical participant in the frisk. Now, with the throne nearer his grasp, he is less often in Falstaff's company and on these occasions his detachment is complete. *Times*, 9 May 1951)

If a combination of directorial control and actorly restraint could contain Falstaff's excess as well as the supposed dangers of the tavern–brothel scene, the Gaultree betrayal (IV.i;IV.ii) was apparently more troublesome. 'No longer do we yawn while an undifferentiated crowd of blustering barons keeps us from Falstaff, for the barons are now an element in the design, of equal weight to Falstaff', wrote Richard David (*Shakespeare Survey*, p. 131). But to the *Stratford-Upon-Avon Herald* reporter, Prince John's deception and his (offstage) massacre of the rebels was a 'shocking', 'scarcely bearable' exhibition of the 'worst of the Lancasters' (11 May 1951). By again hypothesising the responses of Shakespeare's audience, scholars might argue that Elizabethan spectators would accept John of Lancaster's treachery 'without enthusiasm but with a sense that war requires it, and that commanders are by nature speciously pious' (Humphreys, p. 238; Sprague, pp. 87-8). Yet however performed, the scene calls Prince John's Machiavellian tactics into question, particularly when he invokes 'Christian care' and God's will to justify his actions against the Archbishop, Mowbray and Hastings. Certainly Redgrave's preparation copy reveals some uneasiness about the contradictions within royal policy posed by the scene, which his staging attempts to compensate for and turn to advantage. Not only does he position Westmoreland and the other royal commanders in the stage-right royalty corner, enforcing their alliance with the king's cause, but he notes, 'we are to suppose that their forces are identified with the audience, who should feel themselves on the side of the King'. Rather than leaving the armies offstage, Redgrave masses both factions on opposing diagonals and reverses the last two couplets of IV.i so that the traitors can be marched off to 'Strike up our drums, pursue the scattered stray; / God, and not we, hath safely fought today' (IV.i.346-7) – lines that Prince John shouts to the back of the audience where 'we are to suppose the main body of the Royal Army is'. Pointed in this way, the Gaultree action and John's words become a parodic anticipation of Agincourt where, once again, a royal commander will claim his victory for God (IV.vii). In assuming a particular 'we' – one who

will unquestioningly uphold the values and practices of the crown –
Redgrave sought to legislate the relationship between spectator
and representation – a strategy which seems less like Prince John's
and closer to that of *Henry V*'s Chorus, who urges spectators to 'eke
out' staged events with a collective imagination prompted by his
celebratory vision of the play's hero. But whether or not Festival
spectators were alarmed at finding themselves surrounded by the
King's forces or reassured to be counted as true subjects remains,
like the responses of the play's first audiences, unrecorded.

In contrast, the so-called Crown Scene, well-known because
frequently anthologised, was by far the most striking moment: 'a
spectacle moving in the extreme' where the production 'reaches its
greatest heights' (*Solihull and Warwick County News*, 13 May 1951;
Berrows Worcester Journal, 11 May 1951). Here, if not at Gaultree,
critics not only perceived the play as part of a larger historical
sequence but, folding their allegiance into Henry IV's spectacle of
rule, read the King's death through an aesthetic of subjective tragedy, expressing their investment in tributes for Harry Andrews's
playing:

> The real heroic link in the first three plays ... is the life and death of
> Bolingbroke transformed into King Henry. Harry Andrews carries the
> epic story, fiery into grey, with unbroken power. Seldom has approach-
> ing death been done with grimmer sincerity, till failing strength has
> quenched even the flashing eye. (*Manchester Guardian*, 10 May 1951)

> ... [T]he dramatic scales were tipped heavily in favour of royalty chiefly
> by the playing of Harry Andrews as Henry. Mr. Andrews' performance
> throughout the three plays ... has proceeded in a high curve which has
> encircled the Lancastrian story with fine feeling. ... Tonight he showed
> the King in decline and beautifully encompassed the tragedy of failing
> strength. Yet as the grasp loosened on the uneasy sceptre, and the royal
> glance faded from the eyes, the leonine head was occasionally lifted in a
> hint of the old dominance. (*Birmingham Post*, 9 May 1951)

> Harry Andrews, who has been proving so strong a fulcrum in this series,
> carried the aged, ailing King along his last troubled stretch with finely
> controlled dramatic power. There has, as yet in these histories, never
> been a more finely acted scene than that between the dying king and
> Prince Hal, played with quiet dignity and sense of feeling by Richard
> Burton. (*Birmingham Mail*, 9 May 1951)

To support what turned out to be the high point of history's 'long
curve', Redgrave not only made the scene a structural climax but
staged it as a sacramental occasion. Once again, a mime carefully
situated locale and mood: scattered figures crossed the bridge,

carrying a canopy with the motif of the Jerusalem Chamber; the central doors opened on to a processional entry, in which the crown and sceptre preceded the King, who was supported by Surrey and a doctor and closely attended throughout. Log-bearers brought on a candlestick with guttered candles, and monks crossed the stage as a distant clock – presumably carried forward to echo the clock in *Henry V*'s opening moments – softly struck eleven once Henry IV was borne into the inner chamber, where slow, sad music continued until he and Hal were alone.

At this point as at few others the prompt copy has frequent underlinings: although such stresses commonly record, for the prompter's benefit, lines that were spoken slowly or hesitantly, here they single out Henry IV's mocking accusations of Hal as well as those lines that rehearse the crown's history and its 'new' legitimacy – emphases which reflect the production's foregrounding of kingship. In addition, the prompt copy registers what must have been a particularly dramatic pause just before Henry, after hearing Hal's report of 'trying' with the crown, turned to him on 'O my son, / God put it in thy mind to take it hence' (IV.iii.306-7).[1] At the last, Henry died surrounded by Warwick, Hal and all his sons; placed on a litter, he became the centre of a processional exit which recalled *Richard II*'s closing moments. Once the procession cleared the stage, the candles went out, and the several remaining supers knelt. The only light came from the fire, which glowed brightly for a moment in homage to both the old and new kings and to the crown that joins them; then, as a distant trumpet sounded a 'twisted, saddened version of the theme most associated with Bolingbroke,' the great double doors to the inner chamber closed and, after briefly picking out the Jerusalem Chamber motif on the central canopy, the stage lights faded to black.

Calling attention to the new ruler, *2 Henry IV*'s final act opened with a short fanfare, during which Henry IV's flag was taken down from the right panoply and hung above Richard II's; brought on by soldiers, Henry V's flag was hung in the topmost position. Although the play now moves to Shallow's Gloucestershire orchard, its inhabitants in this production came under the watchful aegis of three kings. Few Shakespearian places seem as closely attuned to the energies of Elizabethan local culture as this particular 'other Eden',

[1]Harry Andrews's Henry IV can be heard on a 1964 Shakespeare Recording Society *2 Henry IV*, in which similar emphases recur in a surprisingly (for the verse-speaking conventions of the times, which stressed the music of the lines) naturalistic reading. The version was directed by Peter Wood, with music by Neville Marriner.

[36]

peopled with figures who are inseparable from the play's original historical moment but, judging from its theatrical record, have, like Falstaff, transcended it. If *2 Henry IV*'s street and tavern–brothel scenes represent the urban face of the Merrie England myth, Shallow's domain dramatises a sociology of the English countryside that critics and playgoers alike have idealised. In these scenes, so the legend goes, audiences hear the nation's popular voice, speaking in communal harmony. As evidence of Gloucestershire's 'rich country flavour', most reviewers praised the scene-stealing performances of Alan Badel's Shallow – 'more than a ridiculous fribble, he is the shadow of all senile vanity, pomp strutting in an eelskin' – and William Squire's Silence, 'who sang dolefully in his cups with inanimate persistence' (*Stratford-upon-Avon Herald*, 11 May 1951; Kenneth Tynan, *Observer*, 13 May 1951; *Royal Leamington Spa Courier*, 11 July 1951). One critic, however, put what others had read as disruptive over-playing and caricature into another perspective:

[I]t is difficult to see how [the comic scenes] could have been soft-pedalled. Pistol, certainly, was exaggerated, but it was not the fact of exaggeration, but its character that was disturbing. When will producers cease to treat Pistol as a fantastic? He is the common man who tries to weave romance about himself with tags from the stage successes that have enchanted him, and his counterpart to-day would be an addict of 'westerns' and gangster films. William Squire's Silence was a monstrous exaggeration, a looming, lugubrious codfish with vaguely flapping fins; yet the loud expressionless chanting that would suddenly break from him with deliciously comic effect brought release and relief to the scene rather than disruption. It is not caricature but sober realism that bursts the play. Falstaff, Doll, Shallow are a grim antimasque that, in defiance of theatrical convention, refuses to be dislodged by the play proper, and while they hold the stage it is impossible to believe in kingly nobility or the natural attractiveness of order. (David, *Shakespeare Survey*, p. 138)

Yet taking the 'low' characters' realism seriously ultimately made no difference to critics who came with their own preconceptions about the play and who were prepared to accept and uphold Redgrave's 'right royal' interpretation. Whether from London or the provinces, reviewers recirculated familiar notions, judging Redgrave's production in terms of learned, class-based distinctions which served to insulate Shakespeare safely within the realm of high art. On the one hand, they lavished sentimental praise on the immense vitality of Shakespeare's transcendent comic genius; on the other, they offered appreciative tributes of great 'tragic' acting. That critics also found pleasure in imagining themselves connected to English succession history offers further testimony to this *2*

Henry IV's ties to the joint conservatisms of theatrical art and the dominant ideology. And nowhere did the production exploit those ties so aggressively as in Henry V's two remaining appearances (V.ii; V.v), where Redgrave's staging choreographed the play's emphasis on rule to achieve a consolidated audience response.

For Hal's first entrance as Henry V – which amounts, for the assembled courtiers as well as for offstage spectators, to the introduction of a new character – everything at the back of the bridge remained dark; what little lighting there was favoured the royalty corner and, as the new king appeared (dressed in royal robes but not yet wearing the crown), the light built up so that 'he seem[ed] to dazzle'. Once again, blocking suggested connections to past plays: the courtiers stood in precisely the same positions as in *Richard II*'s court scenes, but, although Henry's entrance was identical to Richard's, the new King's manner of acknowledging his court was in marked contrast: he did not, as Richard had, sit on the throne. The prompt copy marks pauses before the Lord Chief Justice's initial greeting, before Henry's reassurances, and before the Princes' 'We hope no other from your majesty' (V.ii.62) – to which Redgrave added a line for Clarence, 'We do no otherwise than we are willed' (from *1 Henry VI*, I.iii.10). All seemed designed to stress the awkwardness of the moment and, in the case of the added line, to hint at compelled rather than willing obedience. Later on, the pauses surrounding 'rotten opinion' in Henry's vow to 'mock the expectation of the world, ... frustrate prophecies [and] raze out' (V.ii.125-6) popular as well as fatherly rumours pointed the new King's own mockery of his brother-peers and the Lord Chief Justice. Further textual changes reshaped the central encounter between Henry and the Lord Chief Justice. Redgrave deleted Henry's references to his own son and to living to speak his father's words, nor did this Henry promise to 'humble [his] intents' to the Justice's 'well-practis'd directions' in choosing 'noble counsel' or anticipate a future nation-state unequalled in war or peace (the cuts affected lines 103-12, 119-21 and 135-9 in the New Temple edition). A double rationale seems to inform these cuts. Not only did they intensify Henry's decision to name the Lord Chief Justice 'a father to [his] youth' (V.ii.117) and so even more directly parallel Falstaff's rejection, but, by smoothing out traces of the future within Shakespeare's history (including references to a successful nation–state in which contemporary Britons might take nostalgic pleasure), they reserved such matters of governmental policy for further development in *Henry V*. Yet this reshaped accession also suggested that royal authority can contain and regulate all contradictions. The final sign of that occurred when, after naming his new father in the royalty corner, Henry crossed the stage to include John of Lancaster, Gaultree's royal commander, within his newly created family of rule. And for the tetralogy as a whole, a revised Epilogue removed all mention of Henry's son and future loss in order to unite all four plays and perfectly enclose the history they dramatise under the Festival's commemorative umbrella. Written by Patric Dickinson, the new Epilogue broke off at the second quatrain's 'By which the world's best garden was achieved' and continued as follows:

> And nourished there the red rose of his blood
> Awakened from the self-despising dream
> Of tavern victories hallowed by Sir John
> He moves in his true measure: so our theme
> From Richard's winter builds this summer throne;
> Which oft our stage hath shown; and for their sake,
> In your fair minds let this acceptance take.

Given the tetralogy's emphasis on kingship, it was hardly surprising that Redgrave's closing scene exploited Henry V's entry, the most fully dramatised of any coronation in Shakespeare's histories, as a spectacle that entwined royal with theatrical magic. Transformed by bunting and flags, Moiseiwitsch's timbered setting 'blossom[ed] ... abundantly into warmth', and rose petals rained down on the royal party as they crossed the bridge from right to left and descended to the main stage (*Manchester Guardian Weekly*, 17 May 1951). While not as resplendent as that of an 1821 Covent Garden production designed as an 'accurate' reconstruction of George IV's coronation, the entry itself had, for one reviewer, 'the excitement of a real royal procession' (Odell, II, p. 166-9; *Stage*, 10 May 1951). His voice rising above ringing bells and gunfire, Falstaff broke through the barriers enclosing the jostling crowd towards Henry, who paused at the stage-left landing, and the Lord Chief Justice moved protectively to the King's other side. Framed by his two 'fathers,' Henry stared straight ahead as he spoke the rejection, wearing the impartial mask of one who is neither man's son but, instead, their king. Finally, Falstaff himself was framed by the play's two representatives of the law, Shallow and the Lord Chief Justice, as John of Lancaster looked on from the upstage-left corner to oversee his arrest before coming forward to speak this version's last rumour concerning the coming war in France. Two supers placed a new covering on the downstage-right throne and, after John and the Lord Chief Justice exited, three more entered with Henry V's banner, helmet and shield, closing the play with the familiar image which, for this tetralogy, linked beginning to ending, reign to reign, substituting for the play's own Epilogue an emblem of royal deeds to come and, perhaps, alluding to Britain's Allied European victory, most recently commemorated in Laurence Olivier's 1944 film of *Henry V*.

Managed by interpretive strategies designed to stress textual unity and coherence, Redgrave's *2 Henry IV* benefited most obviously from cycle presentation – 'its own autumnal moments', in A.C. Sprague's words, 'preparing for the spring of Agincourt' (p. 91). If it is now possible to re-view the Festival tetralogy as perpetuating the mythos of an England as still powerful (and powerfully intact) and so to read Redgrave's productions as representing less what Shakespeare 'intended' than what Shakespeare was thought to be at a particular moment in cultural history, *2 Henry IV*'s reviewers seemed entirely absorbed by pageantry which Queen Elizabeth I might well have recognised as like her own strategies for ensuring public consent. Although Michael Warre, who played Hal to Ralph Richardson's memorable Falstaff in the New Theatre's 1945 *2 Henry IV*, had regularly burst into offstage tears following the rejection (O'Connor, p. 125),[2] apparently it was not necessary to re-educate Festival spectators to accept Hal's turning away from the fat knight:

> Prince Hal, whose true integrity as played by Richard Burton we have never doubted, retains our allegiance as he finally casts off his low company and emerges as the new king of brilliant promise. Falstaff ... continues in his ways of lovable roguery, but with occasional moments of frightening apprehension, and, at the time of his 'rejection' by the new King, an overwhelming, bewildered sadness. (*Evesham Journal*, 12 May 1951).

> I got ready to blush at the second most loathsome scene in all Shakespeare – the newly crowned Henry V publicly humiliating his former crony, Falstaff, with the words: 'I know thee not, old man!' Then Richard Burton acted the scene with such youthful dignity and fine distaste for his duty as to lift it on to a higher plane altogether. Mr. Burton almost sets the seal on his previous promise as our most interesting young actor for years. (*Evening Standard*, 9 May 1951)

[2]The prompt copy for the New Theatre's *Part One* survives and is in the University of Bristol archives, but that for *Part Two* has been lost.

Amid an overall rhetoric of redemption which identified the actor with his role, only one reviewer – writing that Burton's Henry 'rapidly develop[ed] into that heroic prig who is the next king in the sequence' (Alan Dent, *News Chronicle*, 9 May 1951) – was cynical about Hal's (and Burton's) ability to recuperate kingship as theatre.

Indeed, many lamented having to wait ten weeks for *Henry V*'s opening night: a 'handsome, clean-cut performance that offers rich promise for the larger sequel to come'; 'Richard Burton ... showed clearly that it would have been well worth watching until dawn came' (*Coventry Evening Telegraph*, 9 May 1951; *Wolverhampton Express and Star*, 9 May 1951). As though anticipating *Henry V*'s Fluellen, Janet Evans of Cardiff's *Western Mail* attributed Burton's success to his Welsh heritage: 'He looks the part to perfection, and jumps right into the affections of the audience' (13 May 1951). Others, however, alluded especially to how Burton's performance touched a national chord. Quoting a member of the company, Kenneth Tynan wrote, 'He brings his cathedral on with him', and praised Burton for revealing 'the mystery and power of which heroes are capable' (*Curtains*, p. 12). Harold Hobson was even more explicit: 'Possibly the most exciting thing that has happened at Stratford since the war is the spectacle of Mr. Richard Burton's Henry Monmouth, a dedicated creature with eyes that now glimmer and now shine, driving his way to a splendid royalty' (*Sunday Times*, 13 May 1951).

While such remarks certainly can be read as the early stirrings of a star actor's personality cult, it seems curiously appropriate that a play which closes with legitimating a king served, in this case, to enhance an actor's theatrical reputation. Such a phenomenon is, of course, not new, nor is it particular to the 1951 Festival season. In terms of Shakespeare's own acting company, playing kings was an occupation that could transform marginal men into substantial citizens who – to cite Shakespeare's own case – might even purchase lands and titles.

III

An idealised resolution like that of Redgrave's *2 Henry IV*, which forecloses and absorbs all that Falstaff represents in an 'historical' spectacle centred on the figure of the King, has become a widely accepted theatrical tradition for containing Falstaff's anarchic impulses, especially in productions mounted by Britain's two national theatre companies, both of which currently have (as did Shakespeare's theatre company) royal patronage. Yet the play can be staged to disrupt history's powerful narrative and deconstruct its closing ceremony. Consider, for example, a production that differs in style and ideological emphasis, staged by an Italian company, La Compagnia del Collettivo, Teatro Due di Parma, at London's Riverside Studios in 1983. The programme notes sketch out a view of Shakespeare radically different from the usual praise of the celebrated theatre poet:

> To work on Shakespeare in a society where all is in flux and where nothing utopian is guaranteed is to face the theatre (for us, the world) in company with a colleague who is disenchanted, wise, adventurous, ironic, austere, rigorous, roguish, cunning, cynical, trustworthy and prudent – one who will continually stimulate us with poetically suggestive material appropriate to an 'unnailed' reality as contradictory as our own. [my translation]

Given the company's materialist emphasis, their *Enrico IV* offered a unique possibility for research, through improvisations with and on Shakespeare's playtext, aimed at recuperating what they called its historical dialectics. Rejecting interpretive mythologies aimed at reconstructing the social realities of a sixteenth-century holiday world (as in Redgrave's iconic realism and the BBC's naturalistic 'authenticity'), the eight-member company chose instead a postmodernist performance style of cross-cultural montage which juxtaposed Noh and Samurai ceremonies, vaudeville, and street theatre with more naturalistically conceived moments. Throughout, the production reflected on the conventions of its own performance. This was most obvious in the actor who played Hal and who oscillated between functioning inside his role, playing those of others (costumed like Doll, he sat on Falstaff's knee in the tavern), and standing outside all roles, a cynical and ironic commentator.

At the close, Hal walked alone, to the accompaniment of 'Thus Spake Zarathustra', towards the scarlet curtains marking the up-stage area of the rectangular playing space; crowned, he wrapped his father's medallioned robe around him and assumed a fashion-model's pose – an androgynous figure remote from the audience who, perhaps, waits to be admired and photographed. Directly opposite him, far downstage, Falstaff, dressed in the black suit of the stereotypical Mafia don, sat at one of the café tables that identified the stage space as the tavern and at which some spectators also sat. Similarly dressed, the other tavern followers misted the stage with water from spray bottles as Falstaff shook a huge champagne bottle and, urging Hal to join him, called out ' 'Rico, hey, 'Rico!' Immobile, the new king sang 'I know thee not, old man' to Mr Peachum's cynical betrayal song from Brecht's and Weill's *Threepenny Opera*, and Falstaff cried out and collapsed in his chair. But the production ended with an even more Brechtian touch. Doll, who had functioned throughout as a surrogate spectator able to interrupt (if not change) the action, entered, saw Falstaff and, picking up a champagne glass, dashed it to the floor. Crossing upstage to the King, she tried, but failed, to plead with him; and as the lights abruptly went down, the tune of Gene Raskin's 'Those Were the Days' echoed in the darkening space (see Hodgdon 1991, pp. 183-4). Tellingly, it is a woman who intervenes on behalf of Falstaff and the audience and whose voice (as in Shakespeare's text, V.iv) goes unheard. Finally, Raskin's song offers an explanation and, perhaps, a warning: it is nostalgia for a lost past that prevents the possibility of change.

Ultimately, this exhilarating dislocation of textual and theatrical signs is akin to Shakespeare's equally confrontational dialectic between *2 Henry IV*'s source texts – Holinshed, Daniel and the anonymous *Famous Victories* among them. Yet, while praising the production's excitement, immediacy and 'all the world's a tavern' milieu, critics had reservations about an interpretation that threatened to turn the play into an essay:

> Shakespeare in English and Shakespeare in foreign are different animals. Nobody cares if a translation is mucked about with. A British production seeking this degree of license would either have to play against the text to a degree fatiguing to both actors and audience, or paraphrase, which is an abomination. There are those rhythms, prose or verse, and we are stuck with them. (Robert Cushman, *Observer*, 21 August 1983)

In this critic's vocabulary, being 'stuck' with English language rhythms marks a chauvinistic ownership of Shakespeare ('nobody cares if a translation is mucked about with') apparently blind to the Parma Collective's cultural critique. Although any performance of the play finds its own particular way of realising the play's final assertion of royal hegemony and the rejection of Falstaff, this production's theatre of conventions recuperates and re-presents the oppositional energies between King and Clown in terms that expose both figures as actors in that great theatrical lie called history. Who owns history, the Parma production suggestions, is (as it was in 1597) a political as well as a theatrical matter.

CHAPTER III

Reprise: BBC Shakespeare (1979)

'Every thinking of history', wrote Croce, 'is always adequate to the moment at which it appears and always inadequate to the moment that follows.' Similarly, Peter Brook, a director who claims an interest not in history, but, instead, in the aesthetic relations between performances and their audiences, affirms the particularly ephemeral life of theatrical representations: 'A production is only correct at the moment of its correctness, and only good at the moment of its success. In its beginning is its beginning, and in its end is its end' (Brook, 'Style', p. 256). When applied to Shakespeare, both kinds of thinking point to a bard other than the universal one of Jonson's famous epithet, 'not of an Age, but for all time'. Indeed, although the Festival of Britain histories made claims for restoring authorial 'truth' and Elizabethan political vision to the plays, they were very much the result of making a particularly timely use of Shakespeare's cultural capital. Yet in undertaking to preserve the entire canon on television, the BBC/Time-Life Shakespeare series – and most especially those plays, including *2 Henry IV*, filmed under its first Executive Producer, Cedric Messina – grounded its entire enterprise on just such universalist notions of Shakespeare's 'time-lessness'. As the epitome of culture, Shakespeare was thought to transcend the particulars of any cultural moment. Such assumptions operated on several levels and were dictated not only by the BBC's somewhat neo-Aristotelian mission – to inform, educate and entertain – but, more significantly, by the project's American financial underwriters, who insisted on a commitment to 'solid, basic'

Shakespeare which conformed to 'straightforward' traditional production values that could withstand the test of time (Messina, p. 8). The series was not geared to sophisticated theatregoers or, for that matter, to sophisticated television-viewers; backers feared that 'wild' or 'experimental' versions might compromise the plays' 'maximum acceptability to the widest possible audience' and so also endanger their investment as well as their future profits (which, as it turned out, were considerable). Still other factors contributed to this curious mix of commercialism and aesthetics. In order to make the plays fit already established television time-frames, productions could run no longer than two and a half hours; moreover, all were to be of 'high quality' – performed 'by some of the greatest classical actors in our time' and set either in Shakespeare's time or in the historical period in which the events dramatised took place (Willis, pp. 10-12, 53, 93; Holderness, 'Radical Potentiality', pp. 192-7). 'Accessibility' and 'acceptability' became popular watchwords for adapting Shakespeare to a mass medium of communication over a seven-year period – a project not entirely dissimilar to that of London's public theatres during the final decade of the sixteenth century, when theatre itself was a relatively 'new' mass medium and when (with the exception of *Henry VIII*) Shakespeare's English histories were staged.

That these somewhat constraining premises were eventually either turned to advantage (by Jonathan Miller) or countered (by Jane Howells in particular) has been explored in detail elsewhere (see Bulman, Willis, Holderness). But in terms of the *Henry IV* plays, produced during the BBC Shakespeare's second season, the original precepts governing the series were still rather strictly enforced. In rethinking Shakespeare for television, Messina told directors to downplay theatrical conventions and eliminate as much artifice as possible; to be done right, he maintained, the plays must be done *naturalistically* (Bulman, p. 51). Doing them right also meant serving the author and letting the plays speak for themselves – assumptions the director Peter Brook finds wholly suspect. 'If you just let a play speak', he wrote, characterising what he calls deadly theatre, 'it may not make a sound. If what you want is for the play to be heard, then you must conjure its sound from it' (*Empty Space*, p. 43). But, like Redgrave, Messina was entirely willing to identify Tillyard's interpretive frame – by now subjected to considerable qualification from the scholarly-critical community – with Shakespeare's voice. He talked of the histories as 'a sort of curse of the

House of Atreus in English' and proposed filming them in a uniform style which would clarify continuities among them and result in a coherent totality (Messina, p. 137). Nearly three decades following the Festival of Britain tetralogy, the politics behind that staging were to be reified. And by inviting Sir Anthony Quayle to play Falstaff, the televised *Henrys* seemed poised to reproduce, and even pay homage to, their theatrical forebear. Whether one applauds or takes issue with the 1951 Festival's version of 'political Shakespeare', they conjured from the plays a particular, historically situated voice to which the BBC Television *Henrys* append a much-weakened, though not altogether muted coda.

David Giles, chosen by Messina as a director 'adept at dealing with English history and the English character' (*The Forsyte Saga*), set out to film the *Henrys* as a 'semi-documentary'; Giles's designer, Don Homfray, saw the plays as 'Social Histories' (Messina, p. 19, Willis, pp. 19; 206). And indeed, the single comprehensive impression that emerges, in the case of *2 Henry IV*, is that the camera takes a very dutiful journey through the play. Cut to accommodate the two and a half hours' traffic of television, every scene unfolds in order; the only one missing is the arrest of Mistress Quickly and Doll Tearsheet just preceding the coronation entry (V.iv) – a not unusual omission and one presumably justified, as it often is in the theatre, on the basis that it is digressive. For the most part, the camera seems to watch, recording actions within the frame. When camera movements or cuts do occur, they are primarily functional: a dolly-in to close-up or two-shot, a shot/reverse shot to mark an exchange, or the staple BBC-Shakespeare mid-shot of three heads, two in the foreground, one in the background. Only occasionally, as in the crown scene and the accession scene (IV.iii, V.ii; both discussed below), does the camera apparatus intervene to shape an action. Turning briefly to Orson Welles's 1966 film, *Chimes at Midnight*, which explores the *Henrys* as Falstaff's history, makes it possible to sense what is missing, particularly in terms of shot set-ups that distinguish one character's verbal and physical energies from those of another. Consider, for example, the high-angle full shot that establishes Henry IV's cathedral-like court, where the throne is set so that light from clerestory windows defines his austere figure, making him seem remote and inaccessible to his subjects and to Hal (*1 Henry IV*, I.i, III.ii). When he dies in the same space, the camera isolates his bowed head momentarily, and the sanctified aura of that space transfers, with the crown, to Hal

(IV.iii). Or compare the sequence that tracks Hal's last exit from the tavern (II.v), where he cuts through its jostling crowds like a knife, with Falstaff's, which directly follows it and where the camera slows to the fat knight's pace, registering his inability to extricate himself from the laughing faces that seem to trap and mock him, keeping him from the prince. In the BBC production, by contrast, even those scenes set in a street, a courtyard or the forest seem squeezed: 'history' as well as the play is confined, on the small screen, to the shape of rooms.

However much this may reduce the scale of Shakespeare's play to a series of framed enclosures, the emphasis on history taking place in rooms, and most especially in intimate domestic spaces, was intentional. In one sense, it renders a 'truth' that is more historical than Shakespeare's and, by representing a present-day understanding of politics, also caters to the series' imagined audience. Peter Saccio makes the point:

> The politics of Plantagenet England were the politics of a very small class, very nearly a family quarrel, as intimate as it was public. The politics of Shakespeare's time were heavily the politics of plot, of the conspiracies that interested Machiavelli, of Macbeth who kept a fee'd servant in every noble Scottish household, of Walsingham who did the same on a European scale, of the younger Cecil who quietly and carefully paved the way for James I's accession. But equally, if not more so, this backstairs notion of politics is modern. In our age of public relations and image-building, we have good reason to suspect all public statements and to suppose that real political action takes place privately. Our public pronouncements have unstated objectives; our meetings have hidden agendas, our deeds are followed by rationalising remarks from press secretaries, and the real action takes place backstage, in quiet and sometimes unspoken deals. (pp. 210-11)

If such negotiation between Elizabethan and late twentieth-century political strategies represents one 'hook' for television viewers, yet another comes from creating the illusion of a specific time-period through a kind of localised antiquarianism. Costumes, properties and the architectural details and furnishings of interior spaces all convey a sense of 'the real' or, in Giles's phrase, 'how it was'. Braziers; tapestry hangings; stained-glass windows; the cramped, rush-strewn tavern chamber, set with rude stools and benches; the Archbishop's gleaming refectory table, complete with pewter goblets; Henry IV's bed, heavy with deep red brocade: such details register an oddly homey Classic Comics version of an Elizabethan World Picture. Costumes run a limited gamut from brown to russet to shaded greys; Lady Percy's stark white wimple gives away her class and status as surely as Mistress Quickly's soiled one and smudged face tell hers; Doll's vampy red gown, complete with an ahistorical neckline, is the only theatricalised silhouette, serving to mark her as a whore; similarly, an anachronistic shooting-stick appears at Gaultree, where Quayle's gentlemanly Falstaff perches on it for his speech on sherris-sack (IV.ii). Although viewers can certainly derive pleasure from such evocative nostalgia, tailoring *2 Henry IV* to Messina's emphases on naturalism and on erasing artifice and spectacle also positions viewers as passive, unquestioning consumers of a seamlessly constructed televisual reality that naturalises Shakespeare's history as domestic melodrama.

The BBC *2 Henry IV* turns the play into a three-hander for Henry IV, Hal and Falstaff and makes its expansive themes readable on the human face. The opening moments signal this emphasis clearly and economically. Two mute flashbacks – of Richard II offering the crown to Bolingbroke (*Richard II*, IV.i) and Richard's murder (V.ii) – precede a close-up of Henry IV at prayer, his hands encased in gloves, his anguished face scarred with crusty scabs on his nose, cheeks and mouth, the outward and visible signs of his obsessive guilt. Then, hazy mid-shots detailing the final skirmishes of Shrewsbury's Hal–Hotspur combat, accompanied by Rumour's ironically spoken voice-over, yield to another close-up, this time of 'crafty-sick' Northumberland, who seems incredulous, even suspicious of the battle reports until, at Morton's entry, he immediately reads the news of Hotspur's death on the messenger's travel- and battle-stained face. The sick commonwealth, troubled by rebellion and the 'rotten opinion' surrounding Henry IV's heir, tends to be figured in more global terms on the stage, often through spare or drab sets or symbolic properties, such as the rusty cannon and wintry white branches of Terry Hands's 1975 production. Here, where the political is literalised as the personal, disease blemishes the King's face, cripples and weakens his body. Hal's face bears a slowly fading scar (historically, from an arrow wound, though it looks more like a sabre cut); Falstaff's red nose and cheeks, the classic alcoholic's complexion, echo in the much-seedier Bardolph's fiery nose, snaggled hair and facial wens; Shallow nearly faints while demonstrating rifle drill in the summer heat.

Television naturalism rests on the premise of the fourth-wall convention of 'inhabitable' stage sets, which enclose characters within the frame and position viewers as legitimate voyeurs, overhearing what they say. Wedded to the production's emphasis on domestic intimacy, the convention operates to particular advantage in the scenes detailing the northern rebellion. In the Archbishop's council (I.iii), articulated primarily in mid-shots and close-ups, repeated cuts to Lord Bardolph register his growing anxiety at the others' denials of the King's strength. Just as he is about to protest, a glance from the Archbishop silences him; and when the meeting breaks up, the camera moves in on his still-seated figure as the Archbishop, attempting to ensure his support, touches his shoulder. There are, however, exceptions to naturalism, as when the camera holds on a sustained close-up of Lady Percy, speaking most of her eulogy on Hotspur as a meditative aria while looking off frame-right. Although Michele Dotrice's white, tear-stained face and red-rimmed eyes, ghost-like in her grief, make this a startling image, her strident voice and measured delivery seem disjunctive with the small-screen space and so call as much attention to the heightened theatricality of the language as to her psychological state, an effect made all the more noticeable because of Northumberland's subdued, evenly modulated response. Granted, foregrounding her set speech parallels its theatrical enactment, where such speeches emerge from the linguistic texture of the play and demand a listener's special attention. Moreover, one might argue that the sustained close-up gives a spectator precisely what she or he strains to see (and may rent opera glasses for) in the theatre – every nuance of expression on the actor's face. But if privileging Shakespeare's 'immortal words' moved some reviewers (as, in the case of Lady Percy's speech, it did), others complained that this was 'the worst kind of Shakespeare in its deadly reverence for the word and mediocre response to the spirit' (Laurence Christon, *Los Angeles Times*, 9 April 1980). The most obvious instance of such mediocrity occurs at the Gaultree parle. Rather than attempting to convey the growing tension through editing, the camera records the scene in long shots and mid-shots. Not only do the characters stand about rather uneasily in armour amidst real trees, but uneven sound levels make some voices sound like the Shakespearian Shout familiarly known as coarse acting. Ironically enough, on those occasions when language seems to overwhelm the image track and alter the representational mode, the BBC's desire for 'completeness' risks breaking rather than sustaining the predominantly naturalistic illusion.

By contrast, in Welles's *Chimes at Midnight*, where many of Shakespeare's famous (or not so famous) words get blown away in

Gaultree's wind, lost in the echoing spaces of tavern or court, or swallowed up in Jeanne Moreau's Doll (where 'whoreson' sounds remarkably like 'Orson'), language functions both as pre-text and support for the film's extraordinary visual economy. The distinction can be pointed by comparing two versions of Henry IV's soliloquy, 'How many thousand of my poorest subjects / Are at this hour asleep' (III.i.4-31). In *Chimes*, John Gielgud's Henry IV appears in mid-shot, where back-lighting outlines him in profile and details his facial structure; as the camera dollies in, he seems at once luminously regal and deeply embittered. Although here the close-up – and Gielgud's majestic voice – privilege the character's psychological state, the image heightens the remoteness, isolation and asceticism of an intensely private man who internalises the kingdom's cares: they gnaw at him from within, and he tries to speak them away. In terms of *Chimes*'s visual–verbal economy, this is a highly idiosyncratic moment in which artifice, as well as the camera, serves and preserves interiority and subjectivity. As Gielgud's Henry finishes speaking, the camera pulls slowly away, as though to trouble him no further.

Beginning with similar camera movements, the BBC version dollies in on Jon Finch's Henry, who sits on the dais that raises his bed from the floor. He wears a white (pentitential?) nightgown, open at the throat; his wrists and hands are wrapped with stained bandages; arms crossed on his chest, he fiddles nervously with a signet ring. The camera seems as obsessed with the signs of his illness (reconstructed by Elizabeth Moss from illustrations in medical texts) as he is. Required to bear the entire weight of one of the play's major tropes, Finch's is surely the uneasiest head that ever wore the English crown. He is not only guilt-ridden but overbearing, a quality reflected in his loud, brittle vocal performance (again, too large for the space), filled with self-involvement and self-pity. Where Gielgud controls and suppresses the physical signs of his illness to keep it private, Finch lets them overtake and overtheatricalise his performance. Wracked by the past, he willingly inflicts his vision of things on his courtiers, especially Warwick, whose impatience and embarrassment at his sovereign's self-indulgent mannerisms function (potentially) to figure the responses of the viewing audience.

On two occasions, however, Finch's self-obsessive performance (king as actor, for which Derek Jacobi's Richard II provides the absent model) serves both the play and the BBC's readjusted focus on intimate family melodrama. Slumped on the throne, an exhausted Henry, his voice tinged with irony, apologises for his weakness and calls Gloucester and Clarence, who approach quickly, warily obedient, eager to please their father (IV.iii). The King urges Clarence to become Hal's watchdog; chiding him gently, Henry IV seems for once capable of treating his sons with a surprising warmth, which prompts Clarence to say that Hal is not hunting at Windsor, as Gloucester had said, but is in London 'with Poins and other his continual followers' (IV.iii.53). Hearing what seems to have been spoken in open trust, Henry explodes with a tirade ('Most subject is the fattest soil to weeds ... ' [IV.iii.54-66]), and both sons draw back as though struck. Neatly and economically, the moments reveal the royal family's dynamics as a *fort-da* game where intimate confidence is consistently read as political betrayal. For this Henry, kingship cancels out kinship.

Not surprisingly, the same game shapes the crown scene – one of the two most tensely articulated private conversations in this production (the other is between Doll and Falstaff). With Poins and then with Falstaff, David Gwillim's Hal seems edgy and bored with time-wasting; he is condescending to Poins (a neat cameo of this most discomfortable princely confidant), and it is self-serving *noblesse oblige*, not affection, that prompts him to play, not a drawer, but a musician (Sneak's noise). Thus it comes as no surprise when, as he thinks his father dead and bends as though to kiss his forehead, the gesture is interrupted by his sight of the crown, which he reaches forward to take. Placing it on his head in close-up, he rises; and the camera, rising with him, starts to follow him from the chamber but then pauses, returning to frame Henry IV's waking figure. In the subsequent father–son interview, articulated in mid-shots (of Hal) and close-ups (of Henry) in a shot/reverse shot sequence, Gwillim's bent head, narrow face and wide, expressive mouth react to his father's embittered anger, hysteria and denial. The effect is that both father and son experience, in a short space of time, all the stages of dying. And since Henry has placed the crown in his son's lap, his words address both it and his heir across each cut. Finally, the three appear in a two-shot, the crown positioned between them – king and future king, separated yet joined. And the costs of sovereignty are measured, on the one hand, by Henry's histrionics and, on the other, by Hal's rephrasing of his earlier speech, refashioned to please an obsessive father and to negotiate his ownership of the crown by means of a lie.

The accession scene represents an even more intriguing negotiation, this time between intimacy and theatricality. At Hal's first appearance as the new King, six speakers and a number of silent observers participate in what becomes, in the theatre, a highly public exchange. The BBC production, however, articulates the scene as several private conversations contained within a larger communal occasion. Saccio's description perfectly captures its rhythms:

It is almost a theatre scene, with an unusual number of full-length and distance shots, an unusual sense of the dimensions of the room, and three carefully staged entrances (the Lord Chief Justice, Hal's brothers, and Hal). But it is a theatre scene not because David Giles has irrationally changed his style. Giles retains some close-ups (including one very ill-chosen one) to remind us of the subtext. It is a theatre scene because Hal makes it so. When nervously greeted by the Lord Chief Justice, Hal walks past him, turns, and pauses, standing in a posture of deliberate poise with hands clasped and feet together, framed by nearer bystanders, holding the court in suspense, making them wait for his response. After speaking to his brothers, he initiates his exchange with the Lord Chief Justice with a kind of muted pounce designed to sharpen anxiety ('You all look strangely at me ... and you *most*'). Making his accusation, he collects the rest of the court with his eyes ('How might a prince of my great hopes') and spears the Lord Chief Justice with this collected gaze ('What! Rate, rebuke and roughly send to prison ...'). During the Lord Chief Justice's long response, three close-up cuts to Hal's face show a very slight but increasing smile that reveals his satisfaction with the progress of the scene. He then exploits the ceremony with the sword, the handshake, the throne, the greater and lesser spaces between himself and others, and the variety of his own vocal tone, all to elicit the acclamation he receives at the end ['God save the King!' – an added line]. Like a master actor playing an improvisation with sensitive but less experienced colleagues, he draws from them exactly the responses that he wants. He sets their roles and thereby solidifies his own. He achieves his political ends by manipulating the theatre of his relationships. Elizabeth I would have applauded – but not publicly. (p. 212)

Saccio's reading attributes to the BBC scene an understanding of Queen Elizabeth's theatre of power which may well derive more from his own informed spectatorship than from any intentional directorial decision. As with many critics (myself included), his experience of *2 Henry IV* in the theatre colours what he sees and how he interprets this small-screen production. Reading one through the other, Saccio objects (in a footnote) to Hal's whispering 'You shall be as a father to my youth' (V.ii.117) to the Lord Chief Justice in close-up – 'surely a mistaken choice for a formal act with manifest political content' (p. 213). Yet given the choices this production makes, both in terms of character and representational intimacy, there is something nicely considered, even Machiavellian, about this privately spoken reward to Hal's father's, and now his own, appointee. The man who once had embarrassed a prince in public is refused a similarly public acknowledgment of his restitution by the King. After all, as this newly authoritative Henry V well knows, playing at fathers and sons is a risky business.

A rather different aura of theatrical authority empowers Anthony Quayle's Falstaff. If one sort of nostalgia driving the BBC production centres on recapturing (by means of costumes, properties and interior decoration) historical authenticity, yet another memorialises Quayle's reinterpretation of the role he played nearly three decades before. Far from the over-padded, grotesquely made-up caricature of the old fat man, Quayle's Sir John demonstrates the assured craft of a master actor: in several senses, he is this *2 Henry IV*'s most authentic feature. That authenticity derives, at least in part, from a fortuitous correspondence between the conventions and management of spatial relations on the Elizabethan stage and on television. The public theatre's downstage platform or 'platea' was the area where an actor was not only most visible to but could be most intimate with the theatre audience (Weimann, pp. 73-84). Positioned at the margins of the stage, he stood at the centre of the theatrical space and so figured the curiously contradictory place of the theatre in early modern London, physically situated outside the city limits yet occupying the precise centre of the cultural sphere, joined to it through resonant metaphor. 'All the world's a stage', claims *As You Like It*'s Jaques, and even monarchs believed it. Said Queen Elizabeth I, 'We princes, I tell you, are set on stages, in the sight and view of all the world duly observed.' Moreover, attempts to reconstruct Elizabethan performances assign this downstage locale to the speaker of soliloquies or asides, to speakers whose function is to narrate or comment on the action and, most especially, to clowns – either *Two Gentlemen of Verona*'s Launce or *Macbeth*'s porter, who perform the present-day equivalent of a stand-up comic routine, or those figures whose marginal social status affords them a particular, often contradictory, perspective on the order of things.

Falstaff, of course, plays all these roles. Furthermore, he simultaneously stands at the play's centre and, because he is a theatrical fiction, inhabits the margins of its historical plot. He is the only figure who speaks directly to the camera, as to an audience, thus breaking the production's naturalistic bias. In terms of televisual conventions, his position is akin to the news analyst's talking head; the documentary host whose foreground presence reads, for the viewer, the image of which he is a part; the celebrity whose image is identified with and helps to sell late twentieth-century commodities. Because of their foreground position, each of these figures can manipulate the viewer's relationship to the representation, a point that is most obvious when, in close-up, Falstaff reveals his double use of Shallow as a source of money and of anecdotes to amuse Hal (III.ii, IV.iii) and as he offers what amounts to a commercial for sherris-sack (IV.ii) – an analogy Michael Bogdanov's 1987 production also exploits to advantage.

Yet however similar these televisual spatial relations may seem to those of the Elizabethan popular theatre, important distinctions separate the two. In the theatre, the downstage position has considerable radical potential: the figure who speaks from this margin-at-the-centre can, and often does, question what he sees and hears. Television, on the other hand, works largely as a normative vision of 'the real' and seldom questions its own encompassing orthodoxies. When it does, as in Joan Braverman's 1987 *Joan Does Dynasty*, where the feminist critic's image is superimposed as she deconstructs scenes from the series, the radical critique she performs is not aired during prime time but appears at the televisual equivalent of the margins, released as an 'underground' video project. None the less, Quayle's Falstaffian presence, which at times seems ready to step out of the frame and invade the viewer's space, functions somewhat like hers in that his suddenly looming image does interrupt the naturalistic flow of the BBC's 'historical reconstruction' with an authenticity grounded as much in the conventions of popular programming as in those of high-culture products shown on educational television. Perhaps a better analogue for Quayle's Falstaff is the one-hander-docudramas such as Ben Kingsley's *Kean* or Hal Holbrook's *Mark Twain*. In this respect, one further point is especially pertinent. For Falstaff invites viewers into the representation not through sight – as in film, where a spectator identifies with his gaze – but, by means of the conventions of direct address, through sound. After all, television developed from radio, an aural medium, not as an offshoot of film, which originated as moving images without sound (see Taylor; Holderness, 'Boxing the Bard', in Bulman & Coursen).

Like no other actor in the BBC 2 *Henry IV*, Quayle accommodates his verbal delivery to the medium, turning Falstaff's speech back into a present-day equivalent of what Elizabethan audiences may have heard – highly stylised verbal artifice shot through with idiomatic expressions: consistently, Quayle's performance literally releases the rhythms of that language. Although styles of speaking Shakespeare change radically around every decade or so, the point can best be made by comparing his BBC Falstaff to his earlier one, available on the same 1964 Shakespeare Society gramophone recording that features Harry Andrews's Henry IV. Admittedly, a recorded audio performance is exclusively tailored to a listening experience, but comparing the two reveals that, in addition to the traditions of stage business and gesture associated with particular roles, the vocal patterns of a particular actor may be equally tenacious. On the recording, Quayle points the turns of thesis and antithesis in Falstaff's soliloquies with unusual clarity, marking 'Shakespeare's music' in the fashion of the times. But his carefully measured delivery changes once his Falstaff plays off others' verbal energies: the voice rises and falls, interjecting pauses as well as self-interruptive (and unscripted) quirks of speech. Quayle repeats these hesitations and additions in the BBC *2 Henry IV*; they become the trademarks of an extremely flexible vocal performance that plays against the grain of the BBC's ideals of clear, straightforward Shakespeare. If on other occasions poor sound technology interferes with hearing what characters say, Quayle's delivery requires viewers to listen closely to Falstaff's constantly shifting sound levels. And I do mean sound. For this Falstaff speaks a stream of sounds – 'uh, uh', 'hm-hm', 'harrumph', 'arh-har' – extremely colloquial, very pleasant and, on occasion, quite soft. The choice seems equally attuned to character and medium. A man who cannot – because of both his bulk and the constraints of the small screen – practise physical flourishes indulges his capacities in speech. What viewers experience is an unusual affinity between actor and role: rather than Quayle playing Falstaff, Falstaff plays him. Aristocratically accented, filled with British upper-class mannerisms, Quayle's fat Jack seems the manifestation of William Empson's view of Falstaff as the first major joke of the English against their own class system (p. 46).

In his early scenes with the Lord Chief Justice and Mistress Quickly, Falstaff is still *Part One*'s entertainer, cracking out one-liners, playing off the Lord Chief Justice as his quintessentially correct straight man. The BBC production even gives him a background audience of bystanders who crowd round to overhear and appreciate or, later, fill out the scene of his near-arrest, surrounding both Falstaff and Quickly with their pushing elbows and 'unruly' faces. But by the tavern–brothel scene (II.iv), however, he seems weary – seems, in fact, to have already reached that point in the trajectory of his role where, in most productions, the later Gloucestershire scenes take him. The choice serves the production's emphasis on domestic intimacy as well as the character, for Giles channels the scene to figure Falstaff's sexual performance as its central dramatic fact.

When the Hostess asks, 'Will you have Doll Tearsheet meet you at supper?' (II.i.165-6), a close-up of Falstaff's avid eyes and conspiratorial 'No more words' (II.i.167) expresses the old roué's secret sexuality, and the scene begins not with the drawers' exchange (which is cut) but with another close-up, this time of Doll. As Frances Cuka plays her, Doll is a shrewd middle-aged Cockney with few illusions; Quickly needs to make sure that her employee is well (and sober) enough to satisfy her prize customer. Clearly Falstaff expects this to be a private encounter in a private space; but just as he and Doll are about to stop arguing and get on with their business, the interruptions begin. In the theatre, Pistol's heightened theatricality often makes this an expansively busy scene; here, however, the tight focus cramps his grandiose style, and the usual chase is reduced in scope. Falstaff hardly has enough strength to stand up to Pistol's swaggering: after two silly slashes, Pistol is hunted out by Bardolph and the Page, leaving Falstaff gesturing wildly and ineffectively with his sword, breathless with exertion.

But Pistol's particular brand of the carnivalesque and the energy he brings to the tavern community are not the point here. Giles films the scene to highlight its most intensely private moments – those between Falstaff and Doll. The camera articulates their exchange in close-ups and extreme close-ups which catch every apprehensive shudder of the lonely old man who sees his own death waiting out of frame just beyond Doll's shoulder. Seeking reassurance, Falstaff doesn't believe her casual kisses (here, indeed the 'flattering busses' of obligatory passion); but once he manipulates her into claiming she loves him better than 'a scurvy young boy ... of them all' (II.iv.274-5; pause Cuka's), the eyes brighten and twinkle and he becomes the gentlemanly client, willing to pay for his (however limited) sexual pleasure – when his money comes on Thursday.

Whether it is a new kirtle and cap or an old crown, *2 Henry IV*'s father figures exert power through objects, commodifying their relationships by exchanges of property. Yet even this strikingly intimate portrait of Falstaff and Doll is up for public sale, for, in this equivalent of *Part One*'s play-within-the-play, cut-in mid-shots of Hal and Poins register their mocking voyeurism. Almost as though he is grateful for the interruption which prevents any further test of his sexual performance, Falstaff seems overjoyed to see Hal, yet for once his wit falters: 'No abuse ... none' (II.iv.327) sounds unusually defensive. And as the camera angle widens to include the entire ensemble, it is Hal's gaze, not Falstaff's, that organises the space, and Hal's softly ironic '[honest], virtuous, [civil] gentlewoman' (II.iv.330-1), not Falstaff's words, that prompts Doll to pull her dress invitingly off her shoulders. In that this Hal interrupts Falstaff only to sever his own link with such pleasures, he exploits his former companion to solidify, long before the accession scene, his own role. Finally, Giles robs Falstaff of even the promise of an off-camera liaison by concluding the scene, after Hal and Falstaff exit, with Doll and Quickly reminiscing about the 'honester and truer-hearted' (II.iv.388) Falstaff.

Quayle's Falstaff rallies somewhat among all-male company in Gloucestershire, where he stage-manages the raw recruits like an expert ringmaster and where a night-capped Silence, staring with bland-faced disbelief at Shallow's delight in the 'man of war''s jokes, not only marks a change from the desiring listeners of the earlier street scenes but (potentially) reflects viewers' responses as well. Even if Falstaff loses his on-screen audience, however, he comes alive for viewers when, in the close-ups that articulate his soliloquies on Shallow and, later, on sherris-sack (III.ii.297-323, IV.ii.83-121), he seems about to break out of the screen and enter the viewer's space. And in part because the television convention gives Quayle's richly detailed performance extraordinary power during these speeches, Giles's filming of the rejection, which positions Falstaff as part of an ensemble and denies him a close-up, seems all the more reductive.

As he awaits Hal's entry, framed among an eager crowd and contained behind a rope barrier, Falstaff bubbles with anticipation. Then, a cut reveals the coronation procession – a full shot and, then, a mid-shot of Henry V, with his brothers and the Lord Chief Justice in the background, walking straight towards the camera. His shoulder-length hair shorn and completely hidden under the crown, his figure enveloped in the ermined robes of office, Hal is hardly recognisable in majesty's 'new and gorgeous garment' (V.ii.44); even the Lord Chief Justice and John of Lancaster, the most familiar among the other characters, appear as hazy pictures in a portrait gallery in a startlingly two-dimensional, flattened image. When Hal speaks 'I know thee not, old man' (V.iv.47-72), his voice, as T. F. Wharton notes, '[takes] on something of the stilted rhetorical air of his father's, again enhancing the sense that there [is] no such person, no such identity as 'Hal'' (p. 72). Only two brief cut-in shots of Falstaff, attempting to reply, register his presence, and the exiting royal parade momentarily obliterates his figure. Once he reappears, his face is tear-stained and bewildered; very softly, he acknowledges his debt to Shallow and uses his remaining lines to regain his shattered dignity until, at the Lord Chief Justice's command, helmeted soldiers surround him and take him off as he is still protesting his innocence. A laughing Prince John turns away from the spectacle, and, following his exchange with the Lord Chief Justice, the two exit, as soldiers pass across the screen. Much as though Giles was quoting Redgrave's 1951 production, the final image is of Henry V's coat of arms.

Signs of Messina's professed agreement with Tillyardian ideology, which the production certainly absorbs elsewhere, are not, however, skteched in here. Where Redgrave's production sought to establish the emergence of Henry V's new order as the most salient dramatic and historical fact, the BBC production's diminished spectacle offers only the palest reflection of that order. Yet as Saccio points out, the BBC has considerable experience in filming real as well as fictional historical spectacle – expertise that would seem to lend itself to Giles's vision of the histories as social documentary. Thus his decision to theatricalise Henry V's image within an iconic, distinctly non-naturalistic reality, though undoubtedly deliberate, seems somewhat puzzling.

Giles's choices can, of course, be read through the production's insistent emphasis on intimacy, which the rejection plays out as reversal: once Hal is king, the political becomes the *im*personal. Saccio offers a complementary perspective:

> The screen image of the newly crowned Henry V resembles the late portraits of Elizabeth I, where the face is but a stylized oval surrounded by emblems of monarchy. The king is an icon; and sweaty, quirky, living bystanders are given their orders and left to cope as best they may. The appearance of the king (an historical fact of one kind) is a visual

metaphor for the powers and duties of kingship (historical and dramatic facts of another kind), and through it we see their effect upon human beings. (p. 209)

Saccio's reading follows the new historicist argument that power uses Falstaffian misrule to consolidate its own authority, licensing carnival subversion only in so far as it works, ultimately, to authorise the state – a notion as totalising in its own way as Tillyard's order of things. To the extent that Saccio's language speaks on behalf of Falstaff – 'sweaty, quirky, living bystanders', 'human beings' – he identifies the rejection's crucial significance as a character-defining action for both Henry V and Falstaff in which each draws meaning from the other. Yet for me, the BBC 2 *Henry IV* fails to convey the complex negotiation between history and drama this event embodies. Although making Henry V into an emblem may enhance his royal power, it lessens his *dramatic* authority: he becomes a machine, not a man. While this perhaps captures one side of the transformation from holiday prince to working monarch, it victimises Falstaff and, more especially, reduces what I have called the authenticity of Quayle's Falstaff. For his is a performance authoritative enough to need the full panoply of royal rejection. In short, Quayle's Falstaff deserves not, perhaps, a 'better prince', but a better production.

To say that, of course, is to return to the perennial 'Falstaff problem' and, more particularly, to the issue of how far a production will go to call Henry V's official strategy into question. Once again Welles's *Chimes at Midnight* provides a counter-example. For by staging Falstaff's body as its primary site of spectacle, it turns *2 Henry IV*'s royal narrative, as in Hotspur's phrase, 'topsy-turvy down' (*1 Henry IV*, IV.1.82). In the cathedral space where Henry V is crowned, the rejection occurs in a shot/reverse shot exchange consisting primarily of low- and high-angle close-ups and mid-close-ups, from Falstaff's and Hal's points of view, respectively. Aside from *Part One*'s tavern playlet, when Hal played Henry IV, this is the only time that Falstaff looks up at Hal. Two especially striking shots mark this exchange. In the first, as Henry says, 'I know thee not, old man' (V.v. 47), he stands with his back to a Falstaff he clearly knows so well that he does not even need to (and cannot) look at him; and, in the second, as the new King finally turns away from the 'surfeit-swelled' old man to walk between massed banners towards the light, the film cuts to a mid-close-up of Falstaff, whose gaze registers pride in the splendid figure of his 'sweet boy'. When a group of soldiers carrying lances bar his view of Hal, Falstaff moves slowly to stand alone next to a column, speaks with Shallow and, finally, moves out of the shot. As Shallow calls to him, a series of extreme long shots detail his own procession as he walks away from the camera toward the darkened castle ramparts, his bulk growing smaller and smaller in the frame until, within a deep, empty space, his tiny silhouette disappears through a lit archway. Coming towards the camera in the next shot, the Archbishop, Prince John and the Lord Chief Justice remark on the King's 'fair proceeding' (V.v.95); but then Welles counterposes that judgement with its 'fair' results: Doll is arrested, calling for Falstaff, who is ordered to the Fleet; his tiny Page, squirming through the crowd, tells Pistol that Falstaff is sick; and Bardolph comments, 'The King is a good king, but it must be as it may' (*Henry V*, II.i.120). Before the castle battlements, Henry proclaims, 'Now, Lords, for France' and orders Falstaff released from prison – 'We consider / It was excess of wine that set him on' (*Henry V*, II.ii.178, 41-2). By this point, of course, the film has not only repositioned Doll's arrest but exceeded *2 Henry IV*'s scripted limits to pick up *Henry V*'s Falstaffian traces.

Because the play's epilogue – absent in this representation as in Redgrave's and Giles's productions – also looks forward to *Henry V*, it is appropriate to read these vestiges as a substitute for that convention. But Welles's film – later retitled *Falstaff*, presumably not only to reflect its emphasis on his subjectivity but, by tying the title more obviously to Shakespeare, to make it more marketable – continues to explore the contradictions between Falstaff's story and 'history'. In the tavern, the camera follows Poins as he walks past the empty 'throne' (where Falstaff and Hal had both played Henry IV) into the innyard, where he stops beside a huge coffin, resting on a rude cart: 'Falstaff?' 'Falstaff is dead,' says the Page; and, after Mistress Quickly speaks his epitaph (*Henry V*, II.iii.9-25), she watches while Poins, Bardolph and the Page push the enormous coffin through the inn-yard gates across a snow-speckled landscape bounded by the castle's distant walls. The camera slowly booms up to offer an omniscient perspective that traps this procession, in a high-angle extreme long shot, between tavern and court; and Ralph Richardson's authoritatively impersonal voice speaks a pastiche from Holinshed:

> 'The new king, even at first appointing, determined to put on him the
> shape of a new man. This Henry was a captain of such prudence and

such policy that he never enterprised anything before it forecast the main chances that it might happen. So humane withal, he left no offense unpunished nor friendship unrewarded. For conclusion, a majesty was he that both lived and died a pattern in princehood, a lodestar in honour, and famous to the world alway.

Over a slow-motion film loop of a row of soldiers, nobles and clerics, armed and ready for war, standing against the side wall of a church, pennon lances waving in the breeze, muffled drums beat out a rhythm that replaces his words (see Jorgens, pp. 106-21; Crowl, and Andrew for discussions of Welles's film).

Rejected from the court by the King and from the tavern by Death, Falstaff inhabits a no-man's land between the two spaces over which the voice of 'history' presides, circumscribing and displacing Quickly's report of the fat knight's death with excerpts from Henry V's chronicle epitaph. Finally, the film reconstitutes the body, and the hierarchy, of the kingdom in an image that repeats itself endlessly, like the drums that simultaneously sound Falstaff's death-knell and presage the coming war. If Welles's pseudo-Aristotelian complicity with tragedy generates a 'finer end' for Falstaff (the Hostess's phrase), it also remaps the territory framed by 'I know you all' and 'I know thee not, old man' on to Falstaff's body to call Henry V's spectacle of rule into question. When Steven Mullaney writes of Falstaff's rejection that 'what surprises is not the event itself but the fact that the world being cast off has been so consummately rehearsed: so fully represented to us, and consequently, so fully foreclosed' (p. 87), he identifies precisely the rupture between 'play' and 'historical' work that Welles's film reveals in the disjuncture between image and sound – the one recording what history excludes to hollow out the voice of official memory (see Hodgdon 1991, pp. 151-3).

CHAPTER IV

Fathers and sons: Terry Hands (1975)

Are these things then necessities?
Then let us meet them like necessities
And that same word even now cries out on us. (*2 Henry IV*, III.i. 88-90)

I

King Henry's lines make an apt motto for the juncture of cultural circumstances, socio-economic as well as theatrical, which shaped the 1975 Royal Shakespeare Company Centenary Season: *1* and *2 Henry IV*, *Henry V* and *The Merry Wives of Windsor* – a 'Falstaff Cycle' under Terry Hands's sole directorship. Acknowledging the special place of the *Henrys* in Stratford's history, the Company's artistic director Trevor Nunn spoke of the three plays as a 'single masterpiece which needs to be seen together' and, evoking Coleridge, as a 'national epic with a special message of courage to the English in times of gathering darkness, fear and falling empires' (quoted in Beauman, 1976, p. 6). Although Nunn's statements echo Quayle's prolegomenon for the 1951 Festival of Britain season, in 1975 their terms had even more overt topical resonances.

At that time, many of the concerns expressed in Shakespeare's *Henrys* seemed to have cut across history to surface once again as endemic, locally British worries. Where during the fifteenth century Margaret Paston's letters had catalogued her perceptions of England's 'troublous world' and Lord Hunsdon, Queen Elizabeth I's cousin, had prophesied 'the utter ruin of the whole country',

1970s Britons foresaw a similar crisis. With England's rate of economic growth one-half to three-fifths that of other industrialised countries, many imagined the twilight of the British state, a phenomenon they named 'the English disease' and compared to the decline of Spain in the seventeenth century. In 1973, Britain's entry into the European Economic Community began what one commentator called 'a journey to an unknown destination'; by the following year, combined inflation and unemployment brought bitter confrontations between trade unions and Edward Heath's Conservative government, which was finally brought down by the militant action of miners. Swift changes of government and consequent shifts in political representation threatened to divide the South-east, always the seat of power and wealth, from the North and West, turning the country into 'Two Nations' fractured along class and economic lines. All of these circumstances were directly relevant to Henry IV and the northern rebellion. With twentieth-century Britain again split by factionalism – whose consequences had been anatomised in Shakespeare's plays – current debates focused on yesterday's world and on forging from that past a new vision which would carry Britain through (see Paul Johnson, pp. 411, 428-30 and Briggs, pp. 296, 306-13). Remarking on how this preoccupation extended to theatrical representation, the *Guardian*'s Michael Billington wrote that 'the chronicles and comedies now speak to us more clearly and immediately than the tragedies' (30 January 1976).

As in 1951, the *Henrys* lent Shakespeare's voice to the 'necessities' facing the nation. Once again, too, *Henry V* anchored the season. But where Redgrave's notion of Henry as England's 'true hero' had driven the Festival season, this time an entirely different rationale informed the 1975 centenary cycle of 'social histories'. That rationale has its own history, and understanding it both in terms of the Royal Shakespeare Company's development of a particular theatrical practice for staging Shakespeare's English histories and in terms of the then current economic conditions is crucial to situating Hands's productions, contextualising their stylistics and accounting for their reception.

In 1963, shortly after the Company had reorganised under Peter Hall and gained royal patronage, John Barton and Peter Hall had collaborated on *The Wars of the Roses*, a heavily adapted version of the three *Henry VI* plays and *Richard III*, whose ideological underpinnings drew joint authority from Tillyardian paradigms of hierarchical order and from Jan Kott's somewhat reductive view of Marxist thinking: the implacable roller of history crushes everybody and everything. These productions not only turned Shakespeare's histories into eminently marketable theatrical commodities but crystallised a company style which, accounting for individual differences, came to be shared in common by all the directors working at the Royal Shakespeare Company (for the influence of the Berliner Ensemble and Brecht, see McMillin, pp. 58-61). In brief, that style embraced a series of shared assumptions derived from John Barton's approach to verse-speaking, which entailed a new interest in textuality and an emphasis on Shakespeare's language as a medium for conveying dramatic meaning. Rejecting Stanislavskian techniques, rehearsal work aimed at freeing actors to explore the texts in new ways. In the Company's institutional life, this moment can be illustrated by 'Sonnet Saturdays' where company members gathered to work closely on those texts; that work was later formalised and made public on the 1984 *Playing Shakespeare* videos and in Barton's book. To accommodate this renewed emphasis on the actor's centrality, the playing space was again modified, further altering the physical circumstances of performance. Peter Hall's designer John Bury introduced a mock thrust, accentuated by a steep rake. Bury's massive set localised the early histories in a symbolic milieu of rusted iron and steel in which minimal furniture, properties and the actors' costumes were the only vestiges of the overtly realistic stagings of the past. Although Quayle's architectural modifications, and the Festival season productions he and Redgrave mounted, had initiated the shift away from Victorian pictorialism and representational staging, the 1964 season of histories severed the remaining connections to that tradition. The old Shakespeare Memorial Theatre stage was now, Peter Hall declared, 'very frankly a stage – not just an illusionist's bag of tricks' (Addenbrooke, p. 44). In short, Hall and Barton were forging a new tradition, one that would later be characterised as 'directors' Shakespeare', over which the illusion, if not the totality, of Brechtian alienation techniques presided and (according to some) were all too fashionably superimposed on Shakespeare.

During the years between 1964 and the centenary season, two strongly interpretive productions – of *Richard II* (1973) and *King John* (1974), both directed by John Barton – pushed at the limits of the (more or less) consolidated company style established by the

Barton–Hall histories project. Yet another change in the theatre itself complemented this move. In 1972, the thrust was redesigned to edge out even further towards the audience, and two huge wing walls were added in order to mask the enclosural frame of the proscenium arch and so free the playing space, as much as possible, from 'realist' bondage. What Hall had earlier described as a 'platform for the imagination' (Addenbrooke, p. 44) was now even more obviously a *presentational* stage, and what was on view there, according to some, had less to do with Shakespeare than with John Barton's idea of what Shakespeare ought to be. Both productions, however, represented outgrowths of Barton's academic interest in Shakespeare's dramatic language; his adaptations of the *Henry VI* plays had, after all, created pastiche verse and linking passages which were remarkably 'true' to the vocabulary and rhythms of plays that, at the time, were considered as apprentice work, and few had objected (see Hodgdon, *'The Wars'*). Where Barton had appropriated the first tetralogy for Tillyard and Kott, it was Plowden, *The King's Two Bodies*, and medievalism which shaped his thinking about *Richard II* and *King John*. Exceptionally formal and stylised in its staging, his *Richard II* stressed role-playing as a metaphor for royal as well as theatrical power. Its most striking feature – that two actors, Richard Pasco and Ian Richardson, alternated as Richard and Bolingbroke – was echoed in a double-page programme spread juxtaposing positive and negative photographic images of both actors in rehearsal, a mirroring process that, when extended to the production itself, resulted in staging the politics of kingship as a politics of actorly display and theatricalised ritual, finally resolved in a stunning *coup de théâtre* in which both actors framed a glittering golden figure whose face, topped by the 'hollow crown' in which 'Death keeps his court', was that of Death itself.

To the extent that this production abstracted social meanings as theatrical display, it prepared for Barton's *King John*, which was less a revival than a radical reimagining of John's history tailored, as indeed Shakespeare's play had been, to address a particular historical moment. This time, Barton did more than rearrange and adapt Shakespeare: what appeared on stage was a severely altered *texte combinatoire* fashioned from Shakespeare's play, the anonymous *The Troublesome Raigne* and Bale's *King Johan* that also included newly written material by Barton himself. Like his *Richard II*, Barton's *King John* also stressed kingship's theatricality. Six coronation ceremonials marked the ever-shifting terrain of the play's royal politics to invert and dismantle kingship in a production adapted to mirror England's present-day crisis, where soaring inflation and political hypocrisy demonstrated the government's inability to respond to people's everyday needs, fostering a widespread disillusionment with the promises of post-war socialism (see Hodgdon, 1991, pp. 145-7; 35-6). The production's contemporary relevance, however, went largely unnoticed; rather, Barton's attempt to transform *King John* into a perspective glass for the failures and betrayals of mid-1970s British politics was criticised for betraying Shakespeare. What the age of textual scholarship had described in a vocabulary detailing 'actors' interpolations' and 'theatrical contamination' seemed to have come full circle to charge theatrical interpreters with 'directorial interference' that imposed their vision between the 'true' Shakespeare text and the spectator. Significantly, this practice was not perceived as being confined to Barton's work (or to the RSC) but as widespread; and in 1974 John Russell Brown issued a short, broadly influential polemic against 'directors' Shakespeare':

> Current methods of producing Shakespeare's plays in the theatre flatly contradict the explorative and fluid engagement for which they were written. The director gives unity, the actors settle into their roles and the audience is kept in the dark to receive whatever view of the play has been chosen for them. (*Free Shakespeare*, p. 82)

In its way, Brown's advocacy of releasing the plays from directors and returning them to actors was yet another form of Elizabethanism. Barton's own practice straddled both sides of the issue. On the one hand, he seemed a dictatorial *auteur*; on the other – especially in his insistence on freeing the actors to explore verse – he was an advocate for the kind of productions Brown endorses. But one shift in theatrical practice was undoubtedly under way. Where earlier revivalist innovations had focused on approximating early modern *playing conditions* by adapting existing theatrical structures to generate a more intimate relationship between players and spectators, now all emphasis rested on the *player*: he (and sometimes she), and the language of theatre poetry they spoke, were Shakespeare's only 'true inheritors.'

II

The manner in which these various contexts coalesced to produce a 'new' RSC style seems, in this retrospective account, more straightforward and simple than it undoubtedly was. What was clear, ten years after the Barton–Hall histories project, was that the RSC found itself poised to further its explorations of Shakespeare's playtexts and to take that work in new directions. And in England's 1975 stagflation economy, the rising costs of theatrical materials, together with cuts in Arts Council budget support for the Royal Shakespeare Theatre, served, however inconveniently, as liberating pretexts for such work. Or so the story goes, for it is diffcult to discern, in what sounds like a chicken-and-egg fable, which came first: the need to reconsider established Company practices in the light of current critiques or the pressures of economic necessities. Whatever the case, the Company found, in *Henry V*'s opening Chorus, documentary evidence of how Shakespeare meant his plays to be staged. Sketching out the functions of stage, players and spectators, that Chorus mandates 'a theatre of words' where 'actors on a bare stage conjur[e] the audience with language and nothing else' (Nunn in Beauman, 1976, pp. 6-7). Although it was not entirely surprising, given the evolution of the RSC's work, that they would take cues for redirecting their praxis from Shakespeare's language, this move was especially significant in that it privileged their 'house author' not, as Redgrave and Barton–Hall's projects had done, by shoring him up through historiographical criticism but by relocating Shakespeare's 'true intentions' in his own state-ments of *theatrical* practice. The burden of finding what Trevor Nunn called the 'over-all style and solution' to Shakespeare's thea-tre of discipline fell to Terry Hands. For the first time since the old provincial festival days, a single director would have sole artistic control.

Hands was ideally suited to assume the task of mounting a season of what was later called, in an ironic bow to Grotowski's experimental workshop theatre, 'Poor Shakespeare' (Thomson, p. 151). Like Barton and Hall, he held a university degree in English literature, though it was not from Cambridge but Birmingham, where John Russell Brown had been his tutor. Like Brown, Hands was convinced that turning directors' Shakespeare towards strong ensemble work was essential to furthering the Company's organic approach to Shakespeare's language. Consequently, he brought together, for the frugal 1975 season, twenty-four men and four women, many of whom remained with the Company throughout the next seven years when RSC audiences would see Alan Howard (who played Hal and Henry V in 1975) play all of Shakespeare's

English kings (except John and Henry VIII) in productions directed by Hands. Coming to the RSC from a Liverpool non-proscenium theatre, where he had learned to work without scenery and to fill a theatrical space using only actors and costumes, Hands had put these strategies to use when, during his first years at the RSC, Hall put him in charge of Theatregoround, a branch of the institution that toured flexible, small-scale, relatively low-budget productions to halls, community centres and schools. If at the moment such experience perfectly served the Company's economic exigencies, it also raised questions about how small-scale Shakespeare might fill the Royal Shakespeare Theatre's vast stage. As it turned out, however, Hands's particular brand of 'Poor Shakespeare' was not only (fairly) cheap but undeniably spectacular.

Where Quayle and Redgrave had chosen to observe the plays' chronological order, Hands reversed it to open the season with *Henry V* – in his view, a play about improvisation, interdependence and unity, qualities essential to the ensemble playing he espoused. Although the decision puzzled those critics whose expectations had been shaped by previous tetralogies, Hands clearly stated his reasons: not only was *Henry V* 'a bald, magnificent statement of intent', but since it 'contains *Henry IV, Parts 1* and *2*, it may readily precede them' (Hands, in Beauman 1976, p. 16). Furthermore, Hands saw this reordering as a move that would enable the Company to work on *1* and *2 Henry IV* 'as Shakespeare wrote them to be performed' (Bryden, in Beauman 1976, p. 247). 'Performed' is the operative word here, for what drove all three *Henrys* was the idea of role-playing, an emphasis appropriated from Barton's *Richard II* and stressed in the programme notes, which included extracts from St Augustine, B. F. Skinner, Macready, Oliver Goldsmith, *Hamlet*, Sartre, Beckett and Erving Goffman on acting, role-interaction and performance. 'Shakespeare', wrote Ronald Bryden in a justificatory programme essay, 'imagines for his hero an education that is an actor's education – the rehearsal of an infinite variety of roles in preparation for the greatest role of all.' In such a scheme, *2 Henry IV*, and especially its final scene, becomes redefined: putting aside Falstaff is not the last step to Hal's maturity, and the play ends, as Hands put it, 'with acted majesty which then needs redefinition in *Henry V*' (Hands, in Beauman 1976, p. 16).

Acting majesty in accord with *Henry V*'s instructions required, of course, a bare stage. Capitalising on the structural changes made in 1972, Hands's set designer Farrah constructed not a 'wooden O', but a massive platform with a one in twelve rake; no masking hid the backstage walls, and the lights hung from a huge square clearly visible over the platform, which was framed by two high catwalks at right and left stage. Recalling Peter Brook's 'white box' for his 1970 *Midsummer Night's Dream*, Farrah's design extended Brook's notion of positioning an 'empty space' with doors on a platform stage so that, now, the stage platform – painted black, not white – had become that space. Arguing for the suitability of such a stage on the grounds that the *Henrys* are medieval not only in subject matter but in stagecraft, Bryden's programme essay spoke of the need to rescue the plays from pageantry (they already had been) and place them in a 'bare metaphysical arena in which the soul of a royal Everyman discovers his destiny and true friends'. At first, however, reviewers found it daunting. While Felix Barker complained that the set looked 'like half a concrete bridge over the M40' (*Evening News*, 25 June 1975), Michael Billington dubbed it 'the aircraft-carrier stage' (*Guardian*, 25 April 1975), a phrase that not only captured Farrah's idea of 'launch[ing] actors into the audience' but implied that they were 'clearly defined and metaphorically stripped' (Beauman, 1976, p. 35). On such a stage, actors could, and did, look monumental: if not literally a 'kingdom', it was certainly a stage of power which forced a heightened awareness of the *physicality* of theatrical communication. Furthermore, in Hands's view a play included more than dramatic language: actors' bodies, scenery, lights and music were equally crucial elements of its 'theatre poetry'. Putting this into practice meant giving particular attention to 'the space in which the actor worked and the light that hit him in that space' (Hayman, p. 88); scenes were played out in vivid cross- and overhead lighting (Bryden, in Beauman, 1976, p. 245), accentuating physical as well as spatial relationships and distinguishing moments of absolute convention from those that demanded more naturalistic treatment. By drawing selectively on the accumulated stylistics of past RSC stagings of history, Hands pushed the Company's eclectic mix of Shakespeare, Brecht, medieval ritual and role-playing in a direction it had already chosen. The result, which combined sparsity with excess, might best be described as a theatre of images or, even more appropriately, as a high-tech Elizabethanism which substituted, for Tillyard's Elizabethan World Picture, an equally totalising *theatrical* strategy in which the stage was indeed the world.

Reacting against their irritation with the perceived distractions of past productions (especially John Barton's adaptations), reviewers seemed convinced that they were seeing that elusive theatrical commodity, 'straight Shakespeare'. 'Stratford is back to normal Shakespeare', claimed the *Daily Telegraph*'s John Barber:

> The good news is that simplicity has returned to Stratford-upon-Avon. And with simplicity, truth. And with truth, of course, credibility. The Terry Hands production of 'Henry IV, Part One' boasts not a single gimmick. No one wears modern dress. No one invents new lines. In its centenary year the Royal Shakespeare Theatre honours its poet by honouring this text. (25 April 1975)

Apparently, Hands had reached for and achieved a 'new' company style whose time had come. And at least one of Barber's comments was true: no one did wear modern dress. But the rest, especially the notion that Hands's *Henrys* were 'normal' or 'pure' Shakespeare, as a more specific exploration of his *2 Henry IV* will reveal, was largely, like all theatre, a matter of illusion.

III

Towards the back pages of the voluminous 1975 souvenir programme – by this time, part of an RSC production's educational, as well as interpretive, apparatus – is a drawing taken from Robert Fludd's *The Art of Memory* (1619). It depicts a space very like the bare platform framed by three walls, with an up-centre door and one at either side, which spectators saw as they entered the Royal Shakespeare Theatre to see *2 Henry IV*. The caption informs readers that it represents 'the stage of a typical Elizabethan playhouse constructed according to Vitruvius' theory popular in the Renaissance, that all proportions should be based on those of man's body'. Reading Frances Yates's 1966 *The Art of Memory*, Hands had been intrigued by her analysis of Fludd's memory system – a technique of impressing images and ideas on memory by positioning them in 'loci' within 'the figure of a true theatre' and then recalling them by 'travelling' through that space in an orderly fashion. Part of a Hermetic Cabalist tradition of 'memory places' based on the proposition that sight was the strongest of all senses and therefore the greatest aid to memory (pp. 3-4, 320-67),[1] Fludd's theatre of memory offered support for Hands's notions of Shakespeare's plays as 'total theatre'. Spectators, after all, speak of *seeing*, not

1 At the 1975 International Shakespeare Asociation Meeting in Washington DC, Hands discussed his current interest in Yates's work.

hearing, a play; constructing echoing visual images can draw events together in a spectator's memory, fuse idea with image and heighten the cross-references among all three plays. Strikingly, too, Fludd's ideas about the configuration of memory are analogous to Henry IV's recurrent images of his own guilty past; both, in turn, bear some resemblance to Freud's 'Remembering, Repeating, and Working Through', one of the seminal documents of his psychoanalytic method. Hands's decision to open *Henry V* first turned the *Henry IV* plays into what Kenneth Hurren called 'explanatory flashbacks' (*Spectator*, 2 July 1975) which (ideally) would explore the events contributing to Hal's royal identity. With this scheme, the production had announced its debt to processes akin to psychoanalytic recovery. Moreover, Fludd (explicitly) and Freud (always present in a post-Freudian age) are especially pertinent to understanding Hands's directorial rhetoric of stage images and the obviously Oedipal framework of his *2 Henry IV*, which resulted in a production that might be called a structuralist's dream.

What critics found especially remarkable was the production's visual clarity. That so many reviewers reached for physical descriptive metaphors – of which John Barber's '[*2 Henry IV*] has the clangour of a bronze urn hurled down on to marble' (*Daily Telegraph*, 30 January 1976) is a particularly evocative example – suggested their willingness to accept Hands's production on its own terms. Consistently, too, reviewers praised its pace; and, although critics often carp (and certainly had, in the case of John Barton's productions) about what is missing (or badly spoken), most seemed to assume that they were hearing an uncut text. Yet some 650 lines had been cut, most heavily in the scenes dramatising the rebels' plot: the Archbishop's council (I.iii), for example, was cut by half, approximating the Quarto's version of the scene, which omits the Archbishop's lengthy addresses to focus more expressly on the rebels' responses to what can seem the Archbishop's coercion. A brief account of Hands's playing text offers particular insight into these reviewers' comments. For what matters about these somewhat heavy cuts is not that they occurred – company practice at the time regularly deleted 350–400 lines – but how *2 Henry IV*'s playing text evolved. Where once directors had come to rehearsal with pre-established cuts and blocking, Hands's company came prepared to investigate and *test* Shakespeare's language. Central to all rehearsal work was the question, 'What's going on here?' and lines were retained (or cut) according to whether actors thought them necessary to exploring the text in two ways: the *why* – a character's personal and political motives – and the *how* – the language of role-playing (Hayman, pp. 91-6). Rather than prescribing blocking, Hands invited actors to let the text dictate physical and spatial relationships, and the resulting stage moves were not firmly set until the last minute. What went on in rehearsal, then, involved using one kind of information to generate another, a process that produced the *illusion* of completeness by transforming the play's verbal economy into a visual economy.

The prompt copy carefully documents this transformation. At the top of each scene, a rectangle plots out the precise location of actors on the stage and, throughout, further diagrams record each move. Most scenes were played at mid- or down-centre stage, and since only Stuart Leviton's lighting further defined the actors and characterised the space they inhabited, the overall impression was of a series of little worlds (recalling Brecht's white circle of light) unfolding against a surrounding black void. This sense of the bare stage as a barren kingdom was augmented by the production's predominant scenic element: a tangle of gnarled, winter-withered branches which hung suspended at upstage centre, a constant reminder that the play was 'haunted by death, sickness and decay' (Billington, *Guardian*, 25 June 1975). Hands speaks of the branches as scenery *about* the play, a category in which he includes the rusted, chained cannon, spewing forth broadsheets which littered the stage with rumours; the tavern's circular, womb-shaped white carpet, a sign of the barrenness of Falstaff's 'family' home; the autumn leaves strewn across the stage to figure Gloucestershire's gradual fall towards decay and remaining to carpet the floor for the dying Henry IV's massive bed; and the picnic cloth spread in Shallow's orchard for the last party just 'before the snow begins to fall' (Hobson, *Sunday Times*, 29 June 1975). Hands distinguishes these elements from scenery that is *of* the play, such as Falstaff's great barrel-shaped armchair, suitable for a 'tun of man', and the crown, the focus 'of all [Henry IV's] griefs and [Hal's] aspirations' (Christopher Hudson, *Evening Standard*, 26 June 1975). These are elements as essential as the actors' bodies – a 'hideously dilapidated' Bardolph; a Silence crippled with age – and the costumes each wore – Henry IV's heavy furs and long web-like scarf to keep out the cold; the two-foot peacock feather in Falstaff's newly gentrified cap and his scarlet brocade dressing gown; and Doll's 'voluptuously diseased', tarted-up face and Lautrec-like coiffure, sporting a jauntily placed, oversized flower (Irving Wardle, *Times*, 25 June 1975). Redgrave's iconic realism or Giles's social documentary style, where Finch's ravaged face and hands signified the kingdom's disease, provide counter-examples to Hands's motifs, where 'disease' escapes the body and is brushed across all features of this production's stark 'theatre poetry'. Such a restrained aesthetic moves towards expressionism; because nothing which does not signify is admitted, each actor's presence and each object takes on greater theatrical value.

Perhaps the best way to illustrate how Hands's spatial choreography contributes to realising *2 Henry IV* is to catalogue some of the production's visual (and sometimes, in this total theatre, aural) pleasures. The play opened in murky light as twenty actors, all in dark cloaks, rushed on to the stage from all directions and gathered together to form a pyramid. They began to speak Rumour's prologue in unison ('Open your ears' [*Ind.* 1]), but at a drum roll, the speech broke into phrases, spoken by individual actors and carefully orchestrated to convey the fleeting disharmonies of reports (and history). The actors' multiple entrances and circling movements were immediately repeated by the messengers bringing Northumberland the news from Shrewsbury (I.i). Ensuing scenes offer examples of how language dictated the physical shape of a scene: Falstaff's initial encounter with the Lord Chief Justice (I.ii) took shape as a slow-motion chase suited to its geriatric participants, in which both Falstaff's retreat and the Chief Justice's pursuit identified them as antagonists; and in the Archbishop's council (I.iii), when Lord Bardolph's questions and comments were consistently dismissed, he moved away from the others, whose exit left the disaffected Bardolph behind. Mining language for visual images also served comedy, as when, in Mistress Quickly's attempt to have Falstaff arrested (II.i), Fang leapt at him and hung, viper-like, on his neck while Snare entrapped his left leg, and Bardolph tried to pull Fang off as Francis attacked Snare. Seeing this multiple monster, the Lord Chief Justice could find no ready answer to his 'What is the matter?' (II.i.63). Later, as the Hostess's narrative grew more puzzling, all moved to encircle her, as though proximity might aid understanding, which set up Falstaff's 'My lord, this is a poor mad soul, and she says up and down the town that her eldest son is like you' (II.i.106-7) to be spoken over Quickly's head in seeming confidence. Though some critics thought such artifice over-stylised Shakespeare's naturalistic comedy, what went unremarked was how Hands's staging, which gave Falstaff an early exit after what he assumes is his final put-down of the Chief Justice ('tap for tap, and so part fair' [II.i.195-6]), turned the Chief Justice's reply ('thou art a great fool.' [II.i.197-8]), spoken from a downstage postion in a pool of light, into choric commentary. Not incidentally, the stage positions of Falstaff and the Lord Chief Justice (as in Redgrave's production) anticipate similar blocking, and Falstaff's similar exclusion, at the close.

Elsewhere, too, actors' costumed presences and their patterned movement, sculpted by lighting, distinguish dialogue from moments of absolute verbal convention, such as set speeches. When Northumberland enters upstage right (II.iii), massive in black armour and a plumed helmet, his imposing figure dwarfs Lady Northumberland and Lady Percy, whose circling movements express their inability to sway him. Then, signalling both a textual and an emotional shift, a follow-spot picks out Lady Percy's eulogy on Hotspur, heightening both her meditative state and its effect on her father-in-law, whose change of mind is further marked by a group exit: dragging her husband's sword, Lady Northumberland and her daughter-in-law surround Northumberland and shepherd him off in the opposite direction from which he entered, as though he has literally been persuaded to take the other way. Hands accords entrances even more privilege. As in the Japanese theatre, especially long entrances permit a character's *presence* to speak on its own, register as the primary dramatic fact and so energise the space. When Hal first appears with Poins, he enters up right, crosses to centre and wanders slowly downstage, making his bore-dom and weariness physical before he speaks of them ('Before God, I am exceeding weary' [II.ii.1]); the prompt copy marks a hold at the top of the scene, indicating that the line was delayed. Two scenes later, Henry IV's initial entrance (III.i) repeats his son's trajectory. Here, however, the King travels slowly downstage along a tunnel of light to speak his soliloquy on sleep, an image that perfectly expresses his isolation. Later, as his sons and Westmoreland gather around him in a wedge-like formation, he moves away from their offered comforts; finally, the others bow and retreat into the shadows, leaving him 'martyred' in a follow-spot for his final line – 'We would, dear lords, unto the holy land' (III.i.104).

Entrances also call attention to how a character's presence can change the existing stage picture and take control of or reorganise its spatial relations. When Falstaff visits Gloucestershire to recruit soldiers in one of the play's most well-prepared-for appearances (III.ii), his circling entrance to Shallow and Silence, who are seated on a downstage bench, parades his city magnificence before the awed country justices. He then quite literally usurps their bench of justice as, in turn, Shallow summons the recruits, who are seated together on an upstage bench, behind which Davey presides. In Shallow's realm, class distinctions are spatial distinctions. Eventually, of course, Falstaff has the stage to himself, speaking a truncated version of Shallow's history – some of its details no longer necessary because spectators have seen Shallow *perform* his singular past, especially in an unusually exhausting caliver demonstration: when he finally fires the musket, straight out at the audience, he falls over backwards. Falstaff's recruiting snares serve as a parodic anticipation of Gaultree (IV.ii) where, as the 'regional rebels cluster like black ravens, to pick the carcass of a king (and a kingdom) who is by no means dead' (John Elsom, *Listener*, 3 July 1975), John of Lancaster makes an even more processional (and presentational) entrance than Falstaff's, repeating the familiar circling pattern, by this time an all-purpose sign for the many ways characters entrap one another. Like an animal, he marks the territory as his, and when he reaches the downstage group of rebels, he forces them to move apart – as Westmoreland had previously done – to accommodate him. Like Westmoreland too, when he vows to redress the rebels' griefs ('And swear here ... ' [IV.i.281-5]) he turns away to face the audience, pointing his hypocrisy before, with ironic pretence, bowing stiffly to the Archbishop ('Upon my soul...' [286]). Finally, at his signal (he puts on his gloves), the iron-masked men accompanying him surround the rebels and 'lunge at the mutinous Archbishop as if they were sticking a pig' (David Isaacs, *Coventry Evening Telegraph*, 25 June 1975) to bring his treacherous counter-plot, so to speak, full circle.

Although John Elsom faulted this (heavily cut) sequence for Hands's tendency to 'stray into ornate symbolism' rather than permitting 'plain, even pedantic, storytelling' to represent the full weight of an England 'about to disintegrate from factionalism and jealous bickering', he as well as other critics were struck by an overall 'mood of unrest that is disturbingly topical' and by how 'all that is melancholy and of sad report ... [came] impressively to life'. Sound also contributed to the production's theatre poetry. The croaking ravens heard by Northumberland (I.i) echoed in the rebels' scenes and again at the close; the chimes began to sound in the tavern–brothel (II.iv) long before Falstaff mentioned them to Shallow (III.ii.211); and the 'leaden gait of heavily armoured noblemen', an especially ominous harbinger of civil turmoil, overlapped and drowned out the rural sounds of Shallow's orchard community: all made connections between one event and another, enhancing a sense of simultaneity (*Listener*, 3 July 1975; *Oxford Mail*, 25 June 1975; *Daily Telegraph*, 25 June 1975). In *1 Henry IV* Hands had enhanced simultaneity in the overlap between scenes by keeping characters from one scene on stage while a new one unfolded. Henry IV had remained upstage to observe Hal and Falstaff in the tavern, and both Hal and his father had watched the Hotspur-Mortimer meeting from the shadows, a strategy that Trevor Nunn's *Henrys* also adopted. Such overlaps occur in Hands's *2 Henry IV*, but only in a minor key. One, in fact – the presence of Henry IV's mourning sons surrounding his bier during Act V's Gloucestershire scene (V.iii) – was cut shortly after the preview (David, *Shakespeare*, p. 194). Nevertheless, one particularly resonant visual echo drew two moments of intense voyeurism together. When Falstaff, presiding over his 'family of the 'dispossessed'' (Gordon Parsons, *Morning Star*, 26 June 1975), gathered Doll on to his lap and admonished her not to 'speak like a death's head' (II.iv.236-7), Hal crouched above him, watching from behind red curtains painted with a Boar's Head. Later (IV.v), 'framed by the guillotine-like structure of his dying father's bed' (Thomson, p. 155), Hal gazed down from behind the crown, placed at the King's head, with a similar sinister relish at yet another impotent father.

IV

Spectators who saw Hands's *2 Henry IV* after his *Henry V* (his own prescribed order) discovered that Emrys James, who had played *Henry V*'s Chorus, now appeared as Henry IV. Curiously, no critic mentions this double, one among several of interest – Clement McCallin's Charles VI and Northumberland, Oliver Ford Davies's Montjoy, Morton and Wart, and Trevor Peacock's Fluellen, Poins and Silence – that span both plays, calling attention to Hands's small-scale ensemble as well as to all three productions' emphasis on role-playing. For Hands, the Chorus–Henry IV double permitted James to '[carry] his identity on from the power and practicality of his revelatory Bolingbroke' to a figure 'whose friendly irony

[76]

provid[es] Hal with the father he so significantly lacked in Parts 1 and 2' (Hands, in Beauman, 1976, p. 24). However forced, this logic suggests that Hal struggles to achieve an identity and a role and, to quote Hands, 'doesn't find his balance until *Henry V*, by learning to make his family as big as his entire army or his kingdom, to make his religion a religion not of obedience and medieval hierarchy but of spirit' (Hayman, *Times*, 3 April 1975). In addition, viewing Chorus as the apotheosis of Henry IV's role also suggests the extent to which all three productions appropriated father–son relations as an important register of meaning.

In Shakespeare, of course, family relations are analogous to those between the King and his subjects and can function not only to anatomise but comment upon the operations of power in both. Yet Hands's production was less concerned with an analysis or critique of kingship than with the social and political shaping of the individual personality. In an interview with Ronald Hayman, Hands spoke of being 'bored stiff with productions that put a political slant on Shakespeare's plays because they are only imitations of a fashion. For me politics is the symptom of a disease not the disease itself. Therefore most political plays for me are concerned with symptoms, not with the true disease.' Situating 'true disease' within the 'human condition', Hands retreats to an essentialist position which subsumes the political in an emphasis on 'universal humanity' (Hayman, p. 101). His pronouncements, however, seem curiously at odds with his production's stylistics, many of which (as the preceding catalogue has illustrated) either borrow directly from Brecht or owe an indirect debt to his theatrical practice. Yet this seeming contradiction disappears if one views Hands's work as a collaborative negotiation between the British political theatre of the 1960s (including RSC practice), which had adopted – and adapted – Brecht's 'epic style', and an attempt to stage a 'politics' of interiority.

That Hands's thinking also relied on psychoanalytic paradigms is hardly surprising. Freud's id–ego–superego triad neatly rehearses the Falstaff–Hal–Henry IV relationship and is difficult to ignore. Hands evokes it by remarking that Hal is 'placed between the self-denial of his father and the self-indulgence of Falstaff' (Hayman, p. 101), by characterising *2 Henry IV* as a play in which sons replace fathers, and by the Henry IV–Chorus double, in which the superego, once dedicated to mythologising his own guilty journey to the crown, survives to mythologise Henry V's greatness. *2*

Henry IV, however, is not the ideal vehicle for pursuing a full exploration of these psychoanalytic strands, for it keeps fathers and sons apart, bringing them together only at the culmination of the Oedipal struggle. To make the phases in that process more obvious, Hands's production marked them structurally. Avoiding both the single interval common in company practice at the time as well as the usual break after the tavern–brothel scene (II.iv), Hands delayed the first interval to follow Henry IV's first appearance (III.i) and took the second (as Redgrave's *2 Henry IV* had done) after his death in a move that created several structural rhymes. Not only did these structural choices enforce the idea of sons replacing fathers, but 'Jerusalem' became a motif that linked all three: Henry IV's desire to go to the Holy Land; his death (ironically) in a chamber of that name; and, at Hal's coronation, the establishment (with a bow to William Blake's lyric) of a metaphoric 'Jerusalem / In England's green and pleasant land.' One corollary effect of this emphasis was that it pushed Falstaff away from the production's *structural* centre. For most reviewers, James's Henry IV occupied that position: *Time Out*'s critic, for instance, spoke of how he '[stood] up to Falstaff, for once, and stamp[ed] his name on [both] plays' (January 1976).

If what characterised father–son relations in Redgrave's Festival production was the unlikeness of father and son and their inability to understand one another, just the opposite configuration showed up in Hands's *2 Henry IV*, where Hal seemed indeed his father's son, sharing character traits (anxiety, 'tetchiness') and feeling (for the crown) despite their estrangement (David, *Shakespeare*, p. 199). In performances praised for their subtlety and intelligence, Emrys James and Alan Howard (with more than a little help from director and designer) crafted a crown scene of extraordinary power. Tracing the trajectory of both actors' performances will give some sense of those moments.

Given the proposition that *Henry V* repeats *1* and *2 Henry IV*, Hal's complete maturity must be delayed – a difficulty Alan Howard's Hal turned to advantage. A highly technical actor who can, with certain inflections, produce electric effects, Howard is well-suited to playing arrogant characters, and his ability to convey introspective states of mind and shifts in mood contributed to a richly detailed performance. With Poins (II.ii), he was moody and melancholic, 'playing with a stick as if it were a metronome and snappishly answering his detractors with "let the end try the man"'

(Billington, *Guardian*, 25 June 1975). Robert Cushman had this to say:

> Hal's first scene is a weary (his word) colloquy with Poins, ostensibly his sole remaining confidant; Mr. Howard aims most of his speeches somewhere past his companion's right ear. Trevor Peacock's Poins is quick-witted enough to deal with routine cynicism ... but this disillusion, which we would call alienation, fazes him. ... 'How shall we disguise ourselves?' is the question, farcically bored, of someone who hardly cares to hear the answer. (*Observer*, 29 June 1975)

Once in Cheapside (II.iv), Hal suggested 'the grinding boredom of a man of large powers who has outgrown his old companions and is only too thankful to quit them in pursuit of the King's business – and any sort of a new life' (John Barber, *Daily Telegraph*, 25 June 1975). Here, too, an extraordinary invention expressed Hal's discontent. Although Brewster Mason's Falstaff seemed, to Cushman as to others, 'softer-centred than he might be; [so that] his bitching at Hal and Poins [was] mellow rather than tetchy', making Hal's anger under-motivated, the performers played the final moments of the tavern–brothel scene as a reprise of *Part One*'s Eastcheap masquerade – Falstaff's revenge for 'I do; I will' (*1 Henry IV*, II.v.486), from which there was no going back:

> [The scene caught] alight when, at the words, 'His Grace says that which his flesh and blood rebels against,' Falstaff literally thrusts [Hal] into the arms of Doll Tearsheet. For a moment Hal might succumb (body-contact must be a rare sensation for him), but military news calls him away, into the play's other world. Falstaff has made him look and feel a fool and there will be no forgiveness. (*Observer*, 29 June 1975)

If what motivated his relationship with Falstaff was electing a father he thought he could control – a process that Howard's Coriolanus would repeat with Menenius in a 1978 production for which work on the *Henrys* prepared the way – Hal found him, in this moment, unsatisfactory. Although *The Spectator*'s Kenneth Hurren thought Mason's Falstaff and Howard's Hal wrong for each other (3 July 1975), that is, in some sense, precisely the point that Hands's *2 Henry IV* was designed to make.

The small size of the 1975 company, combined with Hands's conception of politics as a private family matter, greatly influenced the shape of Henry IV's two appearances. Hands cut Warwick's role altogether, reassigning his lines to Westmoreland, Henry's only remaining attendant lord, and his three sons. Consequently, what Shakespeare's text represents as some semblance of public court life became a series of tense, extremely private conferences in which Henry's own role-playing was, until the crown scene, greatly diminished. In Hands's view, kingship is the ultimate role; and since Henry had dislodged that role by usurping the crown, he was constantly attempting to assume it. Said Hands, 'The only time Henry IV ever falls asleep in two plays, someone comes and nicks his crown, which is what he's been afraid of from the beginning' (Hayman interview, *Times*, 3 April 1975). And as Robert Cushman put it, 'Henry IV himself has nothing to do in the play but die.' But this Henry was, according to Michael Billington, 'not the usual poker-backed versifier but a moody, tetchy, choleric pragmatist whose guiding philosophy (taken up by his son John) is "for nothing can seem foul to those that win"' (*Guardian*, 30 January 1976).

Perhaps inevitably, reviewers compared James's highly emotional, egocentric playing – Richard David called him a 'crabbed, pawky, devious, self-pitying politician, a temperamental exhibitionist' – to Harry Andrews's 'surging command' of the King's role (David, *Shakespeare*, p. 199). Yet even for those who remembered past traditions of 'royal acting,' the crown scene was a passionately climactic duet:

> When Alan Howard as Prince Hal ... tried on the English crown for the first time, I thought the weight would kill him. It is a strange kind of agony that possesses his face; it shifts to accommodate hope, joy, triumph, without ever ceasing to be pain. ... That agonized assumption of royalty is, in every sense, [the production's] crowning moment; and it nails, not just this play, but the triptych of which it is the centre. (Cushman, *Observer*, 29 June 1975)

> [Howard] makes something deeply thrilling of the scene at Westminster, where he first tries on the crown, blinking and squinnying like someone pitched into a room full of light and allowing his voice to acquire a note of iron as he entertains the thought of kingship. Gone is the cliché notion of Hal as the cold-hearted schemer: instead we have a complex man educating himself for monarchy. (Billington, *Guardian*, 25 June 1975)

Hal re-entered still wearing the crown and slowly crossed to his father, who rose on 'O foolish youth!' (IV.iii.225) to confront his son; as Henry IV fell back on the bed, Hal took off the crown ('Thou has sealed up my expectation' [IV.iii.232]) and returned it to his father, who held it close until, on 'bid the merry bells ring to thine ear / That thou art crowned' (IV.iii.240-1), he pushed the crown on to Hal's head, at which the Prince screamed in protest. Continuing his tirade, James's Henry again rose ('Harry the Fifth is crowned'

[IV.iii.248]) and, snatching the golden coverlet from his bed, threw it around Hal's shoulders in a parodic coronation (staged in exactly the same place where, in *Part One*, Hal and Falstaff had taken turns playing king). Then, aping a town crier, Henry leapt on to a chair, descending to crawl along the floor ('the wild dog / Shall flesh his tooth on every innocent' [IV.iii.260-1]) and rising once more to howl out his anger at the thought of an England 'peopled with wolves' (IV.iii.266) before he finally collapsed on the end of the bed. It was only here, according to Richard David, that 'Mr. Howard's defences really [broke]. For a moment he is caught between roles (wanton prince, hero-king) and there is contact' (*Shakespeare*, p. 199).

James's histrionics allowed Howard's Hal to gauge his following speech to undo his father's gestures. Howard used the moments to play with the crown: he presented it to his father ('There is your crown'), he addressed it at a distance ('Therefore, thou best of gold ...') and, finally, facing his father, he took it in his hand ('Let God forever keep it from my head') before placing it on the floor (IV.iii. 271, 289, 303). His actions led to a passionate embrace, and Hal knelt by his father to hear his final advice, which James punctuated with another embrace ('Thou art not firm enough' [IV.iii. 332]), as though transferring his own resolve to his son. Falling to his knees in prayer ('How I came by the crown, O God forgive' [IV.iii.347]), Henry crumpled to the floor; Hal seized him, as though terrified that his father might die before he could respond to him, before he could (legitimately) be *given* the crown. But the exchange never occurred. Rather, Hal reached for the crown ('Then plain and right must my possession be' [IV.iii.351]), gave it to Henry IV ("Gainst all the world will rightfully maintain' [IV.iii.353]), and both rose, Hal helping his father to his feet. And, since the entrance of John and Warwick was cut, the scene ended as Hal picked Henry IV up in his arms and carried him offstage.

In these two performances, the moments just before Henry IV's death became the production's most pointed illustration of Hands's notion that human unity is more important than national unity and thus transcends it (Hands, in Beauman 1976, p. 15). And, although he did eventually cut the intended tableau of mourning with which he had planned to open *2 Henry IV*'s third act, he retained its formal effect for the accession scene (V.ii), where Hal, together with his brothers, stood at the foot of the upstage-centre bier and then walked slowly downstage to confront the Lord Chief Justice. As in both Redgrave's and Giles's *2 Henry IV*s, the scene demonstrated Henry V's ability to enact his new role:

> The habit of play-acting grows on him ... and once king he plays a fearful tyrant for the Lord Chief Justice before forgiving him. This is a faultless interpretation which only fits of manner prevent from turning into a faultless execution. (Cushman, *Observer*, 1 February 1976)

> The only truly moving incident [occurred] when Griffith Jones show[ed] the Lord Chief Justice taking his life in his hands. For he defies the new Henry V and has the courage to defend his past treatment of a Prince he had sent to prison as a mutinous rogue. The King pardons him. The dignity of the old man, and the hard-achieved decision of the young monarch are finely contrasted and built by the two players into a moment of high dramatic crisis. The profligate Prince has recognised, with a kind of desperate relief, how he must bear himself in office. (John Barber, *Daily Telegraph*, 30 January 1976)

V

That reviewers so consistently spoke of Brewster Mason's Falstaff as a figure on his own rather than in relation to Hal (or to his father–king and his father-in-Law) suggests less about his centrality to the play than the extent to which his character remained tangential to Hands's father–son design and to what one critic called 'the Alan Howard show' (Wardle, *Times*, 25 June 1975). Although using *Henry V*, which excludes Falstaff (Fluellen cannot even remember his name), to anchor the season may have contributed to re-situating Falstaff at the margins of family dynamics, including *Merry Wives* (which dramatises a society that lies beyond Agincourt) in the season's 'Falstaff cycle' seemed designed (at least theoretically) to capitalise on Falstaff's centrality. In terms that mediate between his theatricality and his function within the moral narrative of Hal's education for kingship, Hands described Falstaff as 'the most protected character in Shakespeare', one who 'hides behind endless masks' and is 'very rarely an activator of any kind, but ... sets off a constant awareness in other people of how much their salvation depends on themselves' (Hayman, *Times*, 3 April 1975). Yet this more accurately describes the Falstaff of *Part One* than that of *Part Two*; besides, given Howard's highly intelligent Hal (a Prince who already seemed to know too much) as well as *2 Henry IV*'s structure, which tests Hal and Falstaff separately, Falstaff's opportunities to perform such moral work are confined to the tavern–brothel scene and the ending.

Some reviewers, especially those looking for the familiar, expected to see what Quayle had brought to the role – a 'real, unpardonable wickedness' which would justify his rejection:

[Mason's] Falstaff remained a perfectly unobjectionable pet, an amiable sheepdog that any king might continue to have about the palace without scandal. Such a Falstaff may be acceptable in *The Merry Wives of Windsor*, which ends in general reconciliation and a community of laughter, but in *Henry IV* it will not do. Unless the audience understands that Falstaff is in very truth a corrupter of youth and that the Prince is in real danger, the character has no dramatic function and becomes a mere decoration. (David, *Shakespeare in the Theatre*, p. 203)

David's preconceptions, however, blind him to a performance most described in adjective-fattened prose: 'warm and dignified ... a born charmer', 'entirely sympathetic ... magnanimous, seigneurial and valiant', a 'lovable opportunist' (Michael Coveney, *Financial Times*, 30 January 1976; Irving Wardle, *Times*, 25 June 1975; David Isaacs, *Coventry Evening Telegraph*, 25 June 1975). As Robert Cushman observes, this was 'Falstaff seen through the eyes of Mistress Quickly' (*Observer*, 29 June 1975). Stephen Gilbert gives a perceptive account:

The casting of Brewster Mason as Falstaff casts a strong light across the social structure of the play. The first thing to be said is that this Falstaff is a natural aristocrat. We do not for one moment doubt the legitimacy of that knighthood. This man has breeding and makes good use of it. He is at times close by a *noblesse oblige* manner, more often he assumes out of his standing, is forgiven because of it. He makes casual use of menials, treats Quickly with all the thoughtlessness of a man who has never known want. ... He's no fraud. His position has taught him self-indulgence. It's not a gigantic comic performance, rather a precise character creation that snugs in with the production. (*Plays and Players*, July 1975)

Strikingly, Gilbert's vocabulary evokes notions of natural nobility that suggest a 'man of mode' made entirely of manners or, to use Hands's terms, masks. Following the model of Quayle's decayed gentleman, Mason fleshed out Falstaff's 'half-remembered knightly dignity, only showing a perfunctory interest in roistering' (Jack Tinker, *Daily Mail*, 25 June 1975). 'But why', asked Peter Thomson, 'would such a man mix with a ragged Pistol and a Bardolph sensationally suffering from advanced syphilis and drooping boots? By restoring Falstaff to his knighthood, the production isolated his associates' (*Shakespeare Survey*, p. 155). Like David, though for reasons based on a discomfort with mixing class and rank more appropriate to *Henry V*'s Montjoy than to this play, Thomson found Mason's Falstaff 'upsetting'. Restoring dignity (however compromised) to Falstaff certainly swerves away from David's notions of necessary wickedness. To some extent, Thomson's class anxiety points to an emerging pattern in late twentieth-century interpretations of the role. Like Mason's, the Falstaffs of Joss Ackland (1982) and John Woodvine (1987) also located the pleasures and dangers of Falstaff in his aristocratic niceties, the assumed veneer of class privilege.

Although unacknowledged as an influence, Orson Welles's 1966 film, *Chimes at Midnight*, which reads the *Henrys* as Falstaff's tragic history, provides an additional context for Mason's Falstaff, particularly his ability to 'snug in' with the predominantly elegiac mood of Hands's production. For aside from those who noted his single moment of 'cruelty, cowardice and pandar-like lechery as he force[d] Hal and Doll Tearsheet into copulatory union' (Michael Billington, *Guardian*, 25 June 1975), most reviewers saw not an id-figure of childlishly unlimited desires, but 'an ageing Falstaff whose interior gaiety, if he ever had any, is stilled by the thought of the grave' (Harold Hobson, *Sunday Times*, 29 June 1975). Moreover, he seemed most at home in Shallow's social sphere, among the others whose time is running out:

> Mason underplays Falstaff. ... He does not linger on the jokes or the insults, or bluster his way crudely out of trouble. Mason concentrates on Falstaff's humanity, the loving tolerance of the scene at Eastcheap and his gradual recognition of age and approaching death, in the scenes with Shallow and Silence. His cunning is pragmatic, not malicious, and we sense that, when his ship comes home and Hal is king, he plans genuinely to repay his friends. (Elsom, *Listener*, 3 July 1975)

> It is [Mason], as much as anyone, who brings *Henry IV* back to life in the later stages of Part Two. There's a marvellous mellowness about the scenes in the orchard at Gloucester, with autumn leaves sprinkled across the stage, Sidney Bromley's Shallow twittering on about his imaginary past, Trevor Peacock's tiny, arthritic Silence singing ballads, and Mr. Mason all fruity and genial, beaming at the company from above his wine and whiskers, Santa Claus on the razzle. (Benedict Nightingale, *New Statesman*, 6 February 1976)

Given the flexibility of Falstaff's scripted role, Mason's choices represent one option among many. It was not Quayle's, who expressed bored condescension in Gloucestershire, nor was it Woodvine's or Stanton's, whose longing for one more drink went unheeded by a Shallow distracted by Davy's insistence that he attend to domestic accounts. But it was especially appropriate to Hands's production which, like Welles's film, was 'held together by a sense of time, looking back to the past and ahead to the future' (Irving Wardle, *Times*, 25 June 1975). Here, as elsewhere, it was actors' performances that counted:

> [T]he Gloucestershire scenes come splendidly off with Trevor Peacock's arthritic, bent-double Silence – evoking at least three of the seven dwarfs – stealing the honours. But perhaps the production's most memorable image is of three old men on an orchard bench musing on death and reminding us that Hal's perilous education is conducted against the changing seasons, growth and decay, and man's inevitable, reluctant progress to the grave. (Michael Billington, *Guardian*, 25 June 1975)

The last Gloucestershire scene – 'a very good party', in Wardle's phrase – contained the production's most inspired comic inventions. After spreading a white picnic cloth downstage of the centrally placed bench, Davy knelt by it, filled cups with wine, and passed them to Bardolph who, in turn, passed them along the bench to Silence and Falstaff as Shallow, standing behind them, oversaw the merriment. For Harold Hobson, one of Silence's songs made these moments especially poignant:

> He perceives some joke that is hidden from the rest of humanity, and breaks into a raucous song ['Be merry, be merry, my wife has all...' (V.iii.33)] that is happiness undiluted, joy incarnate. So astonishing is this that his companions ask him for an explanation, and he replies, 'I have been merry – twice' with such relish that you would think that to have enjoyed yourself actually on two occasions in a long life is a privilege few could hope to have. This laughter, this song, and the little dance that irrepressibly follows them, are Silence's Agincourt. For him, as for Henry, time is surely short. (*Sunday Times*, 29 June 1975)

Collapsing into ever briefer lyric phrases, Silence rose unsteadily for a final toast ('I'll pledge you a mile to th' bottom' [V.iii.54-5]) but instead wound up on the floor, where he crawled on all fours to the bench and sat next to Falstaff. All then raised their glasses except Silence, who was able to drink only when Falstaff rocked his hooped-up body back and forth in order to get the wine to flow into him, at which point he finally echoed Shallow's last toast ('cavalieros about London' [V.iii.60]), one among several pay-offs to come. For, just as Shallow urged all to 'Lack nothing, be merry' (V.iii.70-1), Silence quite literally fell. Startled by the knock at the door, Falstaff let go of him so that he tumbled to the floor and there began his last fragment of song, which the others' voices turned to a four-part harmony that seemed, for a moment, destined to go on forever.

Repeating the by-now familiar circling entrance, Richard Moore's Pistol, who 'look[ed] and sound[ed] like the incarnation of something primitive discovered by Dr. Leakey at Olduval' (B. A. Young, *Financial Times*, 25 June 1975), leapt on to the bench, where Falstaff joined him, 'to stage their mock play of King Cophetua and the base Assyrian knight, until Silence's head pop[ped] out, like Mr. Punch, from between their legs and ruin[ed] the act' (David, *Shakespeare*, p. 205). Though it was the first ironic echo of the crown scene's climactic moment when Henry IV leapt on to a chair to mock Hal's coming coronation, it was not the last. For amidst the bustle of promises that greeted Pistol's news and energised the group exit, it was Silence, not Pistol, who spoke the final irony. He had again fallen to the floor and, as Pistol shouted 'Welcome these pleasant days' (V.iii.140), Silence echoed (twice) the phrase of song ('Where is the life that late I led?' [V.iii.139]) that cut across Falstaff's (and the others') high expectations. Then, much as Hal had taken up his dying father's body, Pistol gathered up the picnic cloth with Silence in it; and as he swept both offstage at the tail of the procession, Silence's muffled voice was heard once again, this time posing only a fragmentary question, 'Where is it?' – a final signature of his delayed-action comedy and of the scene.

To move from these lovingly detailed moments of 'social realism,' black-clad stagehands now drew a huge white carpet over the entire stage, transforming the intimacy of the orchard's picnic cloth to an abstract 'snowscape'. The upstage-centre cluster of bare branches were now wintry white, and golden rushes were strewn at downstage centre. As the patterned shadows of Shallow's orchard gave way to hard, brilliant light, a tone picked up in the bright trumpets announcing the King's entrance, a travel-stained tavern crew entered first, Falstaff in a carpetbag cloak, red leggings and baggy boots, and formed a ragged line, stage left, with Falstaff furthest downstage. Wearing pure white cloaks blazoned with the scarlet cross of St George, Westmoreland, Clarence, Gloucester and John entered with the Lord Chief Justice, in scarlet robes and a golden chain of office, to stand in a rigidly ordered column, stage right, with the Chief Justice opposite Falstaff across an empty central aisle. Even before Henry V entered, Hands's choices of *mise-en-scène*, costume and blocking separated institutionalised power from its parodic counterparts to predict that the cost of idealising a king depends on such hierarchical division within the kingdom.

When the new King entered (one of the few upstage-centre entrances in the production), the nobles knelt, and Falstaff crossed the boundary between nobles and commons to confront a 'Jove' dressed and masked in golden armour, an emblematic figure of hedged divinity – unapproachable, austere, wearing the glittering symbols of his power like a shield. Ignoring Falstaff, Henry V continued to move downstage; in place of his request that the Chief Justice speak to 'that vain man' and the Justice's warning to Falstaff (V.iv.44-5; both of which were cut), the Justice and Henry's brothers rose to form a barrier that enclosed Falstaff's followers and so further isolated and intensified the exchange between Henry V and Falstaff. When he at last replied to Falstaff's appeals, Henry removed his golden mask, his agonised expression clearly revealing the 'overwhelming private cost of the public office' (Michael Billington, *Guardian*, 30 January 1976). Falling to his knees at Henry's command, Falstaff remained there until the King, followed by the Chief Justice and his brothers, left the stage. Rising slowly, he stood at centre, replacing the *deus ex-machina*-like Hal and isolated even from his companions, who encircled his figure briefly before officers herded them offstage. Then, in an echo of Henry's ceremonial entrance, Falstaff walked slowly up the central aisle between the impassive figures of Prince John and the Chief Justice. Pausing briefly, he stood under the bare branches as a raven croaked out the last 'speech' of this *2 Henry IV*, turning Prince John's bird of rumoured war into a harbinger of Falstaff's future (see Hodgdon 1991, pp. 175-6). Like the production's elegiac last act, this moment seems indebted to Welles's film, which also lingers on Falstaff's presence, sketching out the contradictions his exclusion encompasses. In a sense, Hands's closing stage image also rewrites *2 Henry IV*'s Epilogue. Here, however, the Clown does not address the audience from a downstage position to promise his return. Rather, Hands constructs a coda that suspends Falstaff's figure far upstage – 'he could be dangling in the drying wind,' wrote John Elsom (*Listener*, 3 July 1975) – poised for the exit that will deny him a place in the forthcoming play.

So condensed into a carefully controlled emblematic design, Henry V's spectacle of rule clearly articulates the play's re-formed social and class distinctions to juxtapose Falstaff's barren beggary against Hal's new royalty. Yet critical reactions to this closing 'shock' of spectacle were curiously mixed. Bernard Crick was not alone in faulting the RSC's obsession with gold (Barton's *Richard II* had also featured a shimmering golden cloak at the close) or in reading Hal's garb as a symbol of divine transfiguration inappropriate to one whose father had usurped the crown (*Times Higher Education Supplement*, 12 September 1975). Peter Thomson thought the ending 'a vulgar splash on the otherwise well-conceived picture of the fat kight's downfall' (p. 155); to show his own distaste, the *Leicester Mercury*'s James Daumler commented:

> Henry V appeared at his coronation in armour and robe of such golden resplendence as to send Liberace quivering with inadequacy into a dark corner of one of his wardrobes. It worked. The audience drew breath as one and an awed American lady murmured, 'Oh, where can I get one of those?' (25 June 1975)

In marked contrast, John Barber, who wrote of the crowned Hal emerging 'like a robot, glistening from head to foot in yellow metal, personifying a royalty so splendid that the realm may at last retrieve her greatness', best captured Hands's particular stylistic alchemy: 'England's guilt has turned to gold' (*Daily Telegraph*, 25 June 1975).

Among the many striking images in Hands's *2 Henry IV*, only this final one had an after-history. It appeared – as a colour photograph – on the back of the dust jacket for Sally Beauman's memorial reconstruction of the 1975 *Henry V*. The image of Falstaff's rejection, it would seem, not only remains crucial to thinking about *Henry V* but confirms *2 Henry IV*'s status as a theatrical entertainment that prepares for *Henry V*'s – and Henry V's – 'greatness'. Although *2 Henry IV* has long been considered an example of Shakespeare's 'mature craft' in which he interweaves multiple historical and dramatic source materials, it was not this production but Hands's *Henry V* which was chosen, among other endeavours, to represent the arts in Britain for what the *Daily Telegraph* called an '"artistic invasion" of the United States' (6 February 1976). Given the history joining the two countries, that a production marking the RSC's centenary year could also celebrate America's bicentennial seemed, somewhat ironically, appropriate. Perhaps more significant, however – especially in the light of Hands's professed depoliticisation of Shakespeare – were the resonances of political difference between Britain and the United States that arose from electing Henry V as the man for all seasons. For, whether consciously or unconsciously, a play dramatising the wartime unification of a nation–state and the emergence of an 'ideal ruler' provided, in the wake of the Vietnam War and Richard M.

Nixon's abrupt departure from office, little more than a fantasy resolution for what many perceived as a sick nation, lacking the 'good advice and little medicine' Warwick (speaking to Henry IV in III.i.42) promises will cure it.

CHAPTER V

'The Cheapside plays':
Trevor Nunn (1982)

I

If the 1951 Festival of Britain *Henrys* had attempted to reify a lost Elizabethan picture in order to shore up Britain's historical present, Terry Hands's 1975 productions, built on a politics of 'pure' Shakespearian textuality, barely hinted at the 'Merrie England' nostalgia that marked the earlier history project. Outside the theatre, however, it was another matter. To celebrate the Theatre's charter and to raise funds for its centenary appeal, the Royal Shakespeare Theatre and the market town of Stratford co-operated in staging an Elizabethan Fair. Nine months in preparation, and at a cost of £10,000, it featured a doubly re-enacted royal processional entry: a 'false' Queen Elizabeth I rode on horseback, accompanied by ladies-in-waiting, jesters, pages, men-at-arms and Stratford's town constables, all in period costume; the real Queen Elizabeth II, arriving to participate in the celebrations, took a canal-boat trip from the Theatre to Holy Trinity Church. A huge swan boat glided along the Avon, the site of a river pageant that ended with a battle between three model galleons; also included in the twelve hours of open-air festivities were a seventy-minute medieval joust, falconry and archery displays, a drama and poetry tent, stalls of Tudor foodstuffs and Elizabethan crafts, a barn dance and a *son et lumière* finale. With a minimalist 'Elizabethanism' gracing the RST's main stage, sentimental traces of that other historical past – combined with the distinctly present-day attraction of a discotheque –

remained as tourist commodities to be bought and sold for a good cause (see Holderness, *Shakespeare Myth*, for analogous commodifications of Shakespeare).

A somewhat different celebration of 'the Elizabethan Age' and of the relations between communal and theatrical space marks the social and theatrical contexts for Trevor Nunn's production of *Henry IV*, subtitled in the souvenir programme 'A History in Two Parts'. Its occasion was the long-awaited opening of the RSC's new theatre in London's Barbican Centre complex, characterised by one of its critics as a building that 'must have been spawned during a gang-bang involving Heathrow Airport, a Trusthouse Forte hotel, and two or three motorway service stations' (*New Statesman*, 18 October 1982). If only because they paid homage to Company history, the plays were an obvious choice: fifty years earlier, in 1932, the Shakespeare Memorial Theatre had staged the *Henrys* for a similar theatrical celebration. Looking ahead to this moment, Nunn had already announced that another cycle of histories would initiate the Company's move to the theatre he later described as 'a jewel – set in a concrete sea' (Beauman, 1982, p. 347). Suggesting 'The Cheapside Plays' as a possible umbrella, Nunn remarked, 'Presumably they will need new packaging for that occasion, too' (Beauman, 1976, p. 8).

In retrospect, both Nunn's title – especially because it evokes Jacobean city comedy, which circulates (and critiques) bourgeois values – and the idea of 'new packaging' seem prophetic. For not only was the new theatre situated outside London's traditional theatre district and within the City of London's boundaries, but the RSC presence at the Barbican marked the Company's partial dependence on such local subsidy (together with Arts Council funding) for survival – a situation ripe for tensions between the notoriously philistine city fathers and a somewhat radical theatrical organisation (see Beauman, 1982, pp. 346-51). Completely contained within the Barbican's urban renewal and development project, the new theatre occupied a locale similar to the theatrical spaces of European Renaissance courts, where ducal theatres were equally enclosed in their sponsors' palaces. As Marvin Carlson notes, the site resembles a modern version of such Renaissance theatrical spaces, 'with the supporting prince being replaced by real estate interests using the theatre as a cultural emblem for the enhancement of surrounding commercial property' (*Places of Performance*, p. 97). Yet, although both location and subsidy arrangements pointed to a theatre constructed by, for, and about the reproduction of 'City tastes' and bourgeois values, at least one critic read the choice of the *Henrys* and their production style as an RSC promise 'not to let a posh and privileged position in the City of London compromise its determination to view life humanely, critically and as a whole' (Benedict Nightingale, *New Statesman*, 18 October 1982).

Perhaps the most significant feature of Nunn's 'new packaging' for the *Henrys* was the theatre itself – a 1,166-seat house, curving in a bent ellipse around the oblique angles of a 44-foot-wide stage with a 1:18 rake (now known as the RSC rake) that offered the advantages of both end-stage and open-stage designs. Although the auditorium clearly separates players from audience, no spectator is more than 65 feet from the stage, and the spatial flow of the architecture directs all attention to a stage well suited to the expansive, swift playing style that had become the RSC's signature. Equally pertinent, however, was a 1981 RSC directorial staff decision to increase the Company's investment in production design. That decision seems to have originated from Nunn's acknowledgement that the 1975 RSC season was not only one of the cheapest but also one of its most spectacular, an achievement he attributed to Hands's designer, Farrah, whose 'sleight-of-eye ... hypnotised audiences into listening to the splendour of Shakespeare's words and believing they had seen it' (Beauman, 1976, p. 8). Yet such a move was hardly without contradictions, especially since Nunn's own 1976 *Macbeth*, staged in Stratford's bare, black-box The Other Place and praised for its virtuosity and for freeing the play, was totally devoid of sets *per se*: the concept of enclosing the actors within a 'charmed circle' and sculpting the action with lighting were the primary elements of scene design. Indeed, both actors and directors at the RSC were now more excited by such small-scale work than by main-house productions, where scene design might encumber rather than release a play; and both looked forward less to the Barbican's large stage than to the more intimate theatre (The Swan) then proposed for the shell of the old Memorial.

Such a controversy between 'bare-stage' and 'scenic' Shakespeare, as well as the distinction between going to hear a play (an oral/aural experience) and going to see it, would have sounded familiar to Ben Jonson, who complained bitterly that masquegoers no longer paid attention to his words but were instead attracted only by the spectacle of Inigo Jones's scenery and costumes.

In theoretical terms, the issue involves subverting, through performance, the autonomy of the text, which is perceived as having 'true' power. And to the extent that 'Shakespeare's words' can be thought to be degraded by spectacle, so, too, does the actor's power, as the play's 'true interpreter', supposedly become diminished (see Blau, Clayton). To some within the RSC as well as to purist critics outside the organisation, the decision seemed dangerously regressive. Its worst-case scenario smacked of Victorian pictorial stagings which might once again overwhelm 'pure Shakespeare' and draw attention away from the plays' intentionalities and resources. Yet however much the Company's investment in what some have called 'designer Shakespeare' was occasioned by aesthetic policy, equally powerful – and distinctly commercial – contexts pressed for renewed attention to theatre as a visual art. Nunn himself put it this way: 'For all our good work, for all our discoveries, our insistence on continuity, for all our present audience response, and for all our earnestness, I do not think we have – yet – ensured a future for Shakespeare. We have not yet put that issue beyond doubt' (Beauman, 1982, p. 354). To the extent that ensuring a future meant attracting and retaining new audiences, the choice to invest in spectacle transformed Shakespeare into a late twentieth-century cultural product, one that could lure spectators enticed by other spectacular venues from cinema to rock concerts and sporting events as well as to the more sensual satisfactions of other theatrical representations: Nunn's *Cats* had already proved an immense box-office success, as would the forthcoming *Les Misérables*. In terms of the Barbican productions of *Henry IV*, the most pertinent of these were a series of recent blockbuster films and Nunn's own highly acclaimed 1980 *Nicholas Nickleby* which, just as the Barbican *Henrys* opened, had won New York's Tony awards for best play, best director, best scenic design and best actor.

From about 1977 on, the American cinema had been reinventing spectacle in science-fiction epics such as *Star Wars*, *Close Encounters of The Third Kind*, *The Empire Strikes Back*, *Star Trek – The Movie* and *Alien* (see Neale, pp. 101-5). If at first such narratives seem irrelevant to the *Henrys*, it is important not only to recognise that, for present-day spectators, Shakespeare's medieval–Elizabethan world is just as remote but that it evokes comparisons (especially through shared emphases on individual heroism and weaponry) to these latter-day 'other world' pictures. Moreover, each of these films draws on classically Oedipal structures and themes in which the hero's search for identity figures prominently. *Star Wars'* Luke Skywalker, for instance, seeks the knowledge of Obi Wan Kanobi, who represents the antithesis of his real father, Darth Vader; like Hal, he aligns himself with a 'false' father in order to forge his 'true' identity. Even more importantly, however, what was essential to these science-fiction entertainments was a special effects technology that tested not just the cinema's capacity to create and sustain an entire 'world' but also the spectator's capacity to believe in that world. The theatrical analogue to such technology is, of course, stage spectacle. But this did not necessarily mean a return of the so recently repressed Victorian pictorialism; rather, it involved *reinventing* theatrical spectacle – and doing so in terms that would give audiences the sensual pleasures associated with other kinds of entertainment. At bottom, the aesthetic principle lying behind rethinking spectacle does not differ substantially from that informing the design decisions for Hands's 1975 *Henrys*, and it is even more closely attuned to Nunn's work on a text which also details the shaping of identity – *Nicholas Nickleby* – in a production that had so thoroughly explored, and exploited, how theatrical power has its basis in *narrative* as well as *spectacle*.

However conjectural, these contexts point to the marginal status of Shakespeare's plays among late twentieth-century representations. Certainly, too, the idea of reorienting production values involved some risks. Old plays wrapped in new packages may be a paying proposition, but pandering to popularity and commercialism, potentially at the expense of the traditions that had shaped RSC practice, could work to deny, if not destroy, that heritage. Yet there is something quintessentially Shakespearian about such cultural negotiations. At the risk of conflating two somewhat different practices, re-packaging old plays as new was common for Shakespeare, The Great Adaptor, who found in the anonymous *The Famous Victories of Henry V* a partial ground-plan for *2 Henry IV*'s narrative; and basing a new play on the popularity and commercial success of a previous one has long been one way of describing *2 Henry IV*'s origins. Moreover, whether in Elizabethan or present-day times, tradition – at once a curiously tenacious yet ultimately tenuous entity – has always been a flexible paymaster. And like great kings, great companies can be the makers of theatrical manners.

II

At first sight, John Napier's constructivist set for the *Henrys* certainly seemed a likely entrant in The Spectacle Wars: a heavy acting machine lashed together from roughly textured, often asymmetrically positioned scaffolding and tiered spaces and shapes, it was a non-pictorial embodiment of Elizabethan London as imagined by Eisenstein or Tatlin. Two critics describe its physical features as well as its flexibility:

> Napier's set offers a medieval counterpart of his all-embracing *Nickleby* design: a massive and intricate group of timber constructions, with catwalks, rusting pulleys, roped hatches, which are tricked off laterally to form an ever-changing module of streets, tavern and palace interiors, Shallow's orchard, and the ominous forest where York's party are betrayed. (Irving Wardle, *The Times*, 11 June 1983)

> Napier's design ... is a magnificent folly of balconies, gangways, rotting beams and rusting armour. It is arranged on three huge trucks, hydraulically operated, that can be cleared for battle scenes, lined up and populated like a medieval frieze for the tavern episodes and, most stunning of all, transformed into the streets of London for Prince Hal's coronation procession. (Michael Coveney, *Financial Times*, 10 June 1982)

Here indeed was Shakespeare in the age of mechanical reproduction, evoking nostalgia for the nineteenth century. Yet, unlike the *Nickleby* set, which extended into the Aldwych auditorium and brought the actors close to the audience, producing the illusion of shared experience, this set did not invite participation but instead required a viewer. In that it altered the relationship between staged spectacle and audience and was immediately recognizable in terms of the designer's personal, private style, Napier's set was situated firmly within the category of the postmodern. Furthermore, like the carefully constructed other worlds of cinematic representations, it made an explicit appeal to a meta-narrative – in this case by encompassing the play within a visual and metaphoric context that approximated, and troped, The City. Napier's Babel-towered image of London translated *Henry IV*'s 'strange things' and 'gross terms' into a structure for everyday life, a habitable space for an entire social world within a monumental living machine. *Henry IV*'s spectators had, of course, come *to* the City to see an old play performed by actors who, as they wandered onto the stage before curtain up, attempted to bridge the gap between stage and audience, chatting with spectators and welcoming them to the new theatrical space.

The souvenir programme not only echoed the set's homage to the RSC's new home but illustrated the *Henrys'* wider geography. Its cover featured a closely built, pyramidal cityscape topped by church spires and castle battlements which was also replicated on the souvenir poster. The first illustration, an early map of Britain, was captioned with 'O my poor kingdom, sick with civil blows!'; and the trope of city space was also reproduced in a double-page spread of early modern London, with St Paul's, Gray's Inn, the Barbican, the walls of The City, Fleet Street, Temple Bar, Smithfields, Finsbury Field, Pie Corner and a bank of houses near London Bridge picked out in bright red ink. Also, a *mélange* of quotations suggested reading the production as a deliberate negotiation between the historical past and the present. For together with the usual critical excerpts concerning fathers and sons, Falstaff and the *Bildungsroman* – all explictly inviting the audience into the play's psychology – were quotes from historians of the early modern period detailing corruptions, diseases, urban violence, punishments for felonies and laws governing brothels. And beside these were the words of the Prime Minister, Margaret Thatcher, speaking at Harrogate of a currently sick society made up of 'those who wish to undermine the institutions and values on which we depend ... [and] who are guilty of eroding the respect for the law and values by which society lives' (*Observer*, 28 March 1982). Although the *Henrys* dramatise a 400-year-old historical fiction, the issues they circulate make similarly urgent connections to late twentieth-century spectators. If, as A. R. Humphreys claims, the *Henrys'* 'true "sources" are a whole national life, thought, and language as felt by a great poet', Nunn's production seemed poised, in terms of both its set and the cues provided in the programme, to relocate – and retell – the plays as *social* history.

Because Napier's set generated the impression that *Henry IV*'s characters are locked inside a sequence of events and spaces, it seemed especially apt for conveying how Henry IV, Hal and Falstaff are all contained within or by social institutions and value systems. Yet it also enabled a view of the *Henrys* which dramatically refocused the usual right royal reading of that narrative through a much wider and more complexly segmented lens. Where, two years before, Nunn had turned Dickens's novel into a drama, he now mined Shakespeare's play with an eye to its novelistic scope to create what Michael Billington called a 'panoramic portrait ... of a wracked and divided England ... [and of] a prince symbolically caught between two fathers' (*Guardian*, 11 June 1982). Although this description sounds not unlike previous *Henry IV*s, especially in its obvious reliance on Freud, the differences in Nunn's productions involved more than scale, more than repackaging the plays as a Cheapside commodity. Perhaps the most important distinction came from situating the *Henrys* not as part of a trilogy or tetralogy for which *Henry V* represented a logical end-point, but as a self-contained entity. For Nunn himself, re-thinking the plays for the 1980s meant casting a Hal who would break 'the traditional mould of a delicate, elegantly proportioned 'honey Lord.' ... I've been brooding for years', he said, 'about a physical image of Hal as somebody capable of violence and thug-gery, someone who was already showing some dissoluteness in his physical life, yet whose mental processes belied that appearance.' Gerard Murphy, an actor with a sturdy 'boxer's physique' and 'slightly rakish face' who had spent several years with the Glasgow Citizens, had come to Nunn's attention when Murphy auditioned for Johnny Boyle in *Juno and the Paycock*; in Murphy's risk-taking abilities and dangerous physicality, Nunn saw the potential star quality he needed for Hal: 'there's something about him which is electric, unique, infuriating, intriguing, amusing, special'.

Speaking of his early reactions to Hal, Murphy described him as 'very ambitious, with lots of charm – a dangerous man [who] wants to be king [and] cannot wait for that crown to be on his head' (Francesca Simon, *Guardian*, 4 June 1982). And as it turned out, the repeated delays in the Barbican's opening – Murphy waited for a year and a half after being cast to begin rehearsals – neatly analogised his sense of Hal waiting in the wings. But where Alan Howard's Hal had demonstrated a thoroughly modern, exclusively upper-class *angst* at accepting the necessary burdens of royal re-sponsibility, Murphy's less generalised ideas about the character stressed Hal's entrapment in a role he dreaded. Reading the royal role through his ambitious Irish working-class background and his own father–son drama, Murphy commented, 'It's hard to say to someone like my father, living in the horrors of Northern Ireland as it is now, "Hey, I'm playing Prince Hal with the RSC!" and expect him to comprehend what it means. But at least we have come to respect one another. And that's what this play is about' (Jack Tinker, *What's On In London*, 4 June 1982). Both Hal's rage at having a career chosen for him and his anger at being misunder-stood came through in Murphy's performance, which revealed a young man deeply at odds with both his fathers – barely concealing his inability to reach a father who cares about him only as an heir; needing Falstaff's affections but annoyed by and even resistant to the fat knight's dependency. Desiring something more than either one could give him yet having no choices, Murphy's Hal understood only *after* Henry IV's death what his father wanted for him, yet even then the official role seemed little more than another, if more conventional, public mask.

For John Barber, Murphy's was 'one of the most exciting and original performances at the RSC since David Warner's [1965] Hamlet' (*Daily Telegraph*, 10 June 1982). The comparison was especially apt. Warner's Hamlet had stressed the character's eccentricities, his unconventional behaviour and his rebellion against Establishment rules and regulations (Wells, pp. 34-5). Murphy's Hal was cut from similar cloth. Most of *Henry IV*'s reviewers, however, missed the traditional ruling-class image and its consequent princeliness, as the following comments suggest: 'a physically unprepossessing boy with a mop of greasy blond hair, and a wide untrustworthy mouth opening into fatuous toothy smiles'; 'dressed like a medieval drop out, his philandering with the lower classes never reveals the instincts of majesty that lie beneath the surface'; 'his youthful vigor sometimes suggests not so much a prince riding the bucking horns of a dilemma as John McEnroe trying to decide whether to be a good guy or a champ' (Irving Wardle, *Times*, 10 June 1982; Milton Shulman, *Evening Standard*, 10 June 1982; Jack Kroll, *Newsweek*, 21 June 1982). Only Jim Hiley was alert to the wider political implications of Nunn's anti-heroic casting: 'Murphy begins and continues as, among other things, a high-class lout. As such he ascends the throne with great conviction, proclaiming a Justice that is bound to be unjust and Christian morality that is immoral' (Trussler, p. 58).

Although Hiley's reading perhaps overstates the case, Nunn's production certainly rubbed against the grain of traditional interpretations. For not only did it undermine *2 Henry IV*'s royal coming-of-age myth but it also called government itself into question. Where other productions had assumed it necessary to reject Falstaff in order to ensure the survival and continuity of what Mrs. Thatcher had called 'the institutions and values on which we depend', Nunn's *Henrys* invited spectators to reassess those values, bring them to account. In short, his productions hinted that Falstaff's sometimes full-hearted, sometimes cynical politics might indeed make him at least as good a choice for the times as Henry IV, the Lord Chief Justice or even Mrs Thatcher. That possibility was thrown into high relief by the performances of the family drama's two father figures, Patrick Stewart's rigidly ascetic Henry IV and Joss Ackland's extraordinary Falstaff – 'as formidable and haunting as any we have seen' (Jack Tinker, *Daily Mail*, 10 June 1982). Curiously, few reviewers even mentioned Stewart's Henry IV, except in passing, and among those who did one faulted him for not conveying 'the sense of royalty as an almost intolerable burden'. Most significantly, only one notice picked out the crown scene, which previous productions, as well as their critics, had emphasised; and yet another critic, noting the 'relative ineffectiveness' of Henry IV's famous soliloquy on sleep, complained about the production's 'extrovert bias towards local theatrical effect and the consequent lack of any searching analysis of the nature and cost of power' (Stephen Wall, *Times Literary Supplement*, 25 June 1982). The absence of critical acclaim for the King, however, had less to do with the production's perceived lacks or with the finely tuned restraint of Stewart's intensely disciplined performance than with Ackland's dominating interpretation of Falstaff. Not only did that performance work to turn the familiar family triangle into more of a doubles act, but he 'overtop[ped] expectation [to make] the tragedy of Falstaff eclipse the spiritual progress of Hal' (Michael Billington, *Guardian*, 11 June 1982).

The interpretive strand that sees *Henry IV* as Falstaff's history is most thoroughly explored, of course, by Welles's *Chimes at Midnight*, which, by coincidence, was screened on television several weeks before the Barbican *Henrys* opened. And, although Ackland had not seen the film, he confessed to having put a lot of Welles into his performance:

> The real Orson Welles, I mean, not his interpretation of the part. As a man Welles exploded brilliantly, and then didn't know where to go. Like Falstaff, I believe he could have achieved so much, but it was frittered away. He gives everyone a lot to laugh about and he can laugh at it too. But inside he is crying. He can see the waste, because he is not a stupid man. (Jack Tinker, *What's On In London*, 4 June 1982)

Welles himself, who saw the *Henrys* as a myth of the loss of Eden with Falstaff at its centre, might have been pleased by the reviewers' opinions of Ackland's fat knight, which could apply equally to his own. Irving Wardle, for instance, thought Ackland's performance 'a textbook view of the Lord of Misrule', exuding a 'mask of warmth' which lacked 'fun and variety'; and Milton Shulman concurred, observing that Nunn had 'converted [Falstaff] into a substantial, philosophical, resolute old warrior whose drinking and whoring are merely diversions from his grave way of life' (*Times*, 10 June 1982; *Evening Standard*, 10 June 1982). Admitting that such an interpretation was logical, Shulman none the less complained about the choice:

> [it] 'drain[ed] all the zest and sparkle out of most of *Henry IV*. Joss Ackland's Falstaff is corpulent rather than bloated. His middle is no more grotesque than that of many City aldermen and [Hal's] endearing insults ... appear curiously wide of the mark when applied to a largish, distinguished-looking citizen who does not seem to be over-indulging in either food or drink. Only in the scene with Doll Tearsheet does Ackland let himself go and find some real humour in the role. If Falstaff is not a caricature, he is a dull dog, indeed, and by trying to emphasise his serious impact on Prince Hal, Ackland forfeits his main purpose, which is to get laughs. (*Evening Standard*, 10 June 1982)

Such comments reveal how Falstaff has been most familiarly read (and dismissed) as a clown – a reading that is, of course, more than a little at odds with Henry IV's overwhelming fears of his potential influence on Hal. None the less, it remains a comforting source of critical pleasure, primarily because turning Falstaff into a clown means that he is not 'one of us'. Where reviewers of earlier productions had been quick to note a Falstaff's aristocratic accent and so to extend that distance, Ackland's upper-class tones had distinctly regional and local traces which some found disturbing. When a Falstaff is too recognisably like us ('a middle ... no more grotesque than that of many City aldermen'), he becomes an even more problematic figure, especially when he appears at a venue where the company to which his performer belongs is partially dependent upon city paymasters. While he avoided engaging with such issues directly, Michael Billington nevertheless praised Ackland's ability to reveal Falstaff's contradictory nature and thought his performance a great one precisely 'because he captures the rich duality of the man: he is both what Auden called "a comic symbol for the supernatural order of Charity" and at the same time a hard, brutal, earthbound realist' (*Guardian*, 11 June 1982). The challenges of a new theatre in a new City space, a renewed commitment to stage spectacle (by way of *Nicholas Nickleby*) and, in Murphy's Hal, a somewhat unconventional casting decision were important factors in Nunn's re-examination of the *Henrys*. Together, all these made local, topical demands on spectators' attentions. But the truly distinctive feature of the productions came from Nunn's ability to recirculate and renegotiate the plays' social energies, a strategy that also marked a particular moment of change in their cultural capital when a Falstaff could alert spectators fully to what L. C. Knights once called, with considerable understatement, the 'flawed and unsatisfactory' nature of the public world (see Greenblatt, Bourdieu).

III

Although Nunn's directorial signature lies in his flair for finding theatrical terms for social meanings, such transformations do not occur within a vacuum. On the one hand, any theatrical production is revisionist; on the other, especially within a company like the RSC, each 'new' production also reveals an awareness of, if not a forthright dependence upon, past productions. In Terry Hands's words, 'It's a case of absorbing and inheriting a tradition, and a lot of insights that people have had. ... There is a kind of living tradition to which I think one tries to contribute' (quoted in Billington, p. 61). Moreover, directors make use of and react to their own past work as well as that of others. Certainly Nunn's *2 Henry IV* grew from his *Nicholas Nickleby*; indeed, some critics faulted him for turning Shakespeare into Dickens. And, by focusing on father–son relations with greater psychological depth than Terry Hands's production had done, Nunn's production continued and extended that exploration, making 'old' connections newly available, both those which resonate between *Parts One* and *Two* and those which link the production to its spectators and to their surrounding social text.

One instance of such negotiations between absorption and inno-vation occurs in the opening of Nunn's production, which gave *2 Henry IV* two prologues, each borrowed from its theatrical past. The first picked up an incident from Shakespeare's dramatic source, *Famous Victories* – Hal's arrest for striking the Chief Justice – to which *2 Henry IV* only alludes: Falstaff twits the Chief Justice about it (I.i) and, in the accession scene (V.ii), Hal uses it to accuse, and then forgive, his newly appointed 'father'. As though in homage to the source play, Nunn's production staged an entr'acte presenta-tion of the *Famous Victories* scene where Cutbert Cutter, indicted for the Gadshill robbery, pleads not guilty and wishes to be tried, not by the Lord Chief Justice, but either by Prince Hal or himself.

Hal steps in, announcing that Cutter is his man, gives the Chief Justice a box on the ear and is promptly taken off to the Fleet. (A following scene in the old play meditates on how class distinctions determine the workings of justice: while Cutter is hanged, the Prince is not.) Played in a broad acting style full of wise-cracking asides by a troupe of Interluders made up of cast-members in minor roles and accompanied by musicians with bladders, sticks and a tiny drum, this unexpected bit of street theatre did more than supply the confrontation absent from Shakespeare's text or flesh out one aspect of the father–son drama. For to stage what the play reports as rumour not only aligned Hal with Falstaff as unruly subjects but economically provided a theatrical double-take on the play's ending.

If including the *Famous Victories* incident began Nunn's production with hints of social critique, the Choral presentation of Rumour which followed clearly owed a debt to Hands's 1975 *2 Henry IV*. It also made a retrospective connection to *Part One*'s opening stage images where, as the house and stage lights dimmed to twilight, a flickering candlelit procession of monks, all in white cowled robes, moved slowly downstage behind the King, who was encompassed by the symbolic weight of a gold-embroidered white cope, while the rest of the company filled the set's dimly lit boxlike rooms, walkways and turrets – and watchers as well as participants assembled to sing a haunting *Te Deum*. In *Part Two*, however, the full panoply of that initial processional assembly, which turned Henry IV's obsessive penance into public theatre, was condensed in an emblematic spectacle. Grouped in a pyramidal configuration reminiscent of the programme cover's Tower of Babel, eleven actors wearing cowled black robes and carrying candles, their faces and shapes indistinct in the darkness, delivered the Prologue, speaking its final line ('They bring true comforts false, worse than true wrongs' [Ind. 39-40]) in unison. But where Hands confined Rumour to its scripted locale, Nunn gave it an omnipresent body, if not a voice. Making use of a favourite RSC staging device, he positioned twelve to fifteen people throughout the multi-levelled set; they watched the play's events, observing even its most intimate scenes.

Most obviously, these watchers provided local colour against the backdrop of the set's dark timbers. While some worked – beating carpets, making beds, hauling kegs, carrying trays, painting signs, operating hoists – others simply drifted on to listen. At times, they became stage-hands, moving the huge trucks from one configuration to another. On one level, their presences fore-grounded theatre's collaborative nature, signifying that it is a socially produced artefact. But, although most reviewers read the watchers as Nunn's self-reflexive borrowing from *Nicholas Nickleby*, their constant surveillance also called history itself into question by reminding spectators that many ways of looking at an event may intersect to leave corporeal traces on what is chosen to write, or perform (see Blau). As in Brecht's theory of estrangement, they suggested the possibility that the self-evident 'truth' of an event is not ordained, and that history, however owned and author-ised, is populated with many silenced voices. And on yet another level, this move to hollow out historical representation also made connections to the meta-narrative of the City, where nothing is private and where even the most intimate moments can come under public control. Although dressed as Elizabethans, *2 Henry IV*'s watchers were also identifiable as late twentieth-century city-dwellers, who see encounters from their windows but do not be-come involved: in the postmodern age, history is not something in which one participates but is, instead, a consumer commodity.

Nunn's strategy of embodying rumour had immediate pay-offs for *2 Henry IV*'s first scene, where, as Lord Bardolph (who had left Shrewsbury's battle when it looked as though Hotspur would surely win), the Porter and Morton entered at different levels of the set, Northumberland was surrounded by news that came, quite literally, from all directions. Here, as elsewhere, the set enhanced that image of enclosure. But rumour also functioned in other ways. Later, for instance, the configuration of watchers and listeners during Falstaff's first encounter with the Lord Chief Justice (I.ii) precisely anticipated the positions they took up at the play's end-ing. In addition, the *Famous Victories* prologue gave a fresh charge to Falstaff's remark to the Chief Justice about Hal's boxing his ear ('and you took it like a sensible lord' [I.ii.195-6]), bringing a knowl-edgeable laugh from spectators which enhanced Falstaff's control – he pointed his walking stick at the Justice – and, momentarily, permitted him to stand outside his role. But it was not only the silent populace, located at the margins of representation, who called attention to possibly competing perspectives on events, for Nunn's staging took particular care to energise those who listen to other speakers within individual scenes. When Lady Northumber-land and Lady Percy attempt to persuade Northumberland not to join the rebels (II.iii), this strategy helped Lady Percy to shape her long set speech so that it became not an obligatory, convention-bound meditation on past history but a considered interruption occurring within the more realistically conceived textures of ordinary discourse. As she began, Northumberland sat on a trunk, as though to wait her out; at one point, Lady Northumberland joined him, seeking comfort from his nearness as she listened to her daughter-in-law describe the dead Hotspur's valour. Not only, then, did Lady Percy's words produce a physical change (Lady Northumberland's initial words – 'I have given over; I will speak no more' [II.iii.5] – had distanced her from her husband), but once she saw the two together, she crossed to confront Northumberland, her voice becoming more urgent as she warned him of the Archbishop's strength.

The most stunning pay-offs for the watching presences, however, came at Gaultree (IV.i) and in the tavern–brothel scene (II.iv), both of which demonstrate the obvious, yet often ignored fact, that in the theatre, nothing is more coded than the body. Both also illustrate how Nunn's commitment to serving up almost all of Shakespeare's language in an expanded social context gave fresh emphasis to the idea of the body politic. Evidence of past productions suggests that staging the rebels' plot poses several difficulties. For one, its topical resonances have changed over time, so that what once may have seemed brutal, though politically necessary, has become increasingly suspect; for another, the scenes detailing the rebellion (I.iii, IV.i) include lengthy speeches packed with recapitulative historical grievances. With *Richard II* as part of his 1951 tetralogy, Redgrave had trimmed references to its events from both the Archbishop's council and Gaultree; viewing the play through Tillyardian lenses, he had downplayed Prince John's duplicity and shored up royal authority by urging spectators to identify with the royal forces. Hands had cut both the council scene and Gaultree (which lost over a third of the 349 lines in IV.i) even more heavily and had been criticised for an expressionistic shorthand which reduced politics to an emblematic spectacle centred on John's neo-fascist tactics. More forthrightly than some of his predecessors, Nunn acknowledged that cutting Shakespeare is not only necessary but enjoyable: 'the study exercise of making a slightly different scene from the one that exists on the page by linking certain speeches together or leaving a section out is most seductive' (Berry, *On Directing Shakespeare*, pp. 79-80). Like Redgrave and

Hands, he redesigned the council scene, but his version began with lines from the Archbishop's final speech ('An habitation giddy and unsure / Hath he that buildeth on the vulgar heart' [I.iii.89-90]), summarised the past history of the rebels' present cause and (as Hands had done) judiciously streamlined most speeches, creating the impression of conversational exchange that has become (following John Barton's adaptation of the early histories) the late twentieth-century hallmark for adapting this particular scene. Yet although theatrical tradition certainly supported similar rearrangements in the Gaultree sequence, Nunn deleted only eleven lines, all of which describe the rebels' cause with elaborate metaphors.

Simply restoring lines that had been missing from past productions is in itself hardly remarkable: each production forges its own particular theatrical contract with Shakespeare's text. But where previous stagings had from the first emphasised Westmoreland's ease at manipulating the Archbishop – a strategy that makes rebellion a token disorder and the Archbishop an ineffective, if not naïve, politician – Nunn's staging explored the possibility that the Archbishop spoke not just for a small group of disaffected nobles, but with a popular voice. His troops included an attentive crowd of peasants, one of whom carried the Archbishop's cross; when Westmoreland arrived, another barred his way, waiting for the Archbishop's signal before letting him enter. Arguing his cause, the Archbishop moved among the crowd, enforcing their collective agreement; as he spoke of how the rebels had been ignored ('We are denied access unto his person / Even by those men that most have done us wrong' [IV.i.78-9]), the peasants applauded him. Later, at Westmoreland's promise – 'This offer comes from mercy, not from fear' (IV.i.148) – all clearly mistrusted his official posture. They banged their staves threateningly, provoking Hastings's and Mowbray's questions about Prince John's authority to act on the King's behalf; all seemed satisfied only when, just before his exit, Westmoreland knelt to kiss the Archbishop's hand. Yet as the Archbishop, trying to allay Mowbray's doubts, paused after 'Our peace will, like a broken limb united, / Grow stronger for the breaking' (IV.i.220-1) to invite their response, the crowd seemed less sure of their commitment and hesitated before, one by one, they raised their hands in consent. By embodying what Richard II calls 'the wavering commons', Nunn's staging of the body politic at first empowered the Archbishop's cause and then, with the peasants' hesitation, made it questionable. And in making their (restored) language do persuasive work, both Westmoreland's and, later, Prince John's (also restored) sermonising seemed all the more hollow and their sham of piety more devious – especially when a smiling Prince John knelt as though to kiss the Arch-bishop's hand but instead ripped the official ring from his finger just before his arrest. Moreover, except for the Archbishop's cross-bearer, Nunn's staging excluded popular witnesses from the final parley, marking the difference between the two stages of the Gaultree scene in terms of class to suggest how power authorises itself to speak for the people by playing what looks like a gentle-men's private game.

If, as one critic claimed, Nunn's 'complete' version of the Arch-bishop's rebellion played against the grain of Shakespeare's text (see Wharton, p. 77), that was not the case in the tavern–brothel where, for once, spectators could relish all its words, including the topical references which most productions invariably delete. In an interview with Michael Billington about this very point, RSC direc-tor John Caird observed that topicality occurs at points in Shake-speare's texts where narrative energy lags, gaps which Shakespeare filled by 'min[ing] a richer vein of topical comedy', often continuing it as though 'he couldn't stop or didn't want to stop' (Billington, p. 21). Nunn himself offered no justification, though a careful pro-gramme reader might have noted there a list of Elizabethan cant terms whose inventiveness encouraged connections to present-day idioms from any one of a number of subcultures, from rock to rap. But the more important point was that exploring a *dramatic* justifi-cation for the twists and turns of Elizabethan vernacular restored something like the scene's 'original' rhythms or, perhaps more accurately, permitted an interpretation of those to come through as richly as possible. Miriam Karlin's Mistress Quickly, for example, was so thoroughly steeped in gin that it took considerable effort to pronounce 'swag ... *ger* ... ers' – some form of which she repeats ten times. It took time. But in one sense, much of the scene concerns time-wasting. Certainly in narrative terms, it is almost entirely gratuitous: although anticipated structurally, it is *about* expecta-tion and seems designed to permit both characters and spectators to revel in that alone.

Nunn's 'ravenous eye for behavioral detail' and his 'alertness to social nuance' (Michael Billington, *Guardian*, 10 June 1982) were most strikingly obvious in this scene, which unfolded in the boozy, mellow confines of an upstairs chamber (entered through a stage trap) dominated by what looked like a replica of the Great Bed of Ware, upon, around, under and behind which much of the scene was played out. Among the observers who appeared at all levels of the set were Hal and Poins, who, by taking off Northumberland's luggage, had already become drawer–stagehands. Indeed, the entire scene-shift had the aura of a set-up; after their initial bustle, all the watchers – their faces picked out by David Hersey's beam lighting (a fine, pencil-thin beam adapted for use as moving spotlights [see Rubin, pp. 164-5]) – settled into positions which offered the best sightlines on the bed. The image was that of an entire city peopled by night-time voyeurs. But the scenario they had hoped to see was interrupted by a city-dweller's worst nightmare come true: the possibility that a psychotic sociopath, in the shape of Mike Gwilym's wiry, hyperactive Pistol, might invade one's private space and hold one hostage.

Initially, drink somewhat calmed Pistol's twitchiness, but his advances to Quickly and Doll, speedily repulsed, prompted a chase around the chamber, with the bed serving as both obstacle course and safe haven: although the brave Francis attempted to wrestle him to the floor, when Pistol drew a long double-barrelled pistol ('Where Erebus, and tortures vile also' [II.iv.153]), both Doll and Francis jumped on to the bed. In Gwilym's performance, Pistol's incoherent Marlovian borrowings underscored the character's violence, which he finally turned against himself. Temporarily mollified by drink – and seated in Quickly's bedside rocking chair, which he set in frantic motion – he again grabbed his gun when Doll insisted that he be thrust downstairs and, pointing it at his head ('Then death rock me asleep...' [II.iv.194]), he leapt on to the bed and put the gun in his mouth ('Come, Atropos, I say!' [II.iv.196]). Either to distract him or to ensure his suicide, Bardolph bit his leg, which sent Pistol vaulting to the rocker, where he turned the trembling gun on Falstaff; and when Falstaff, now armed with his rapier (Francis had produced it from under the bed), came too close, he fired wildly: Falstaff struck the rocker, and Pistol sprang on to the bed.

The stage direction which reads, 'Exit Bardolph, driving Pistol out', mobilised the entire community of Peeping Toms in an effort to capture the madman. Throwing the bedcover over Falstaff to delay his pursuit, Pistol dashed up the stairs and across the centre truck to the stage-right balcony, where a somewhat astonished Hal and Poins barred his way; descending to the second level, he was stopped momentarily by another watcher on the stage-right catwalk but managed to evade him by swinging to its front edge, where he brandished his pistol at two more watchers who screamed and scurried downstairs. Now actively pursued by at least six people, including Hal and Poins, he squinnied through the bannisters enclosing the crow's nest, where he was again met by Hal and Poins, who had passed Falstaff (and gone unrecognised). But the elusive swaggerer escaped their grasp and scrambled down to ground level; there, met by Bardolph, Francis and two drawers, he fired his gun one last time, at which they all dropped to the floor. Sneaking up on Pistol, the drawers grabbed him and shoved him feet-first down the trap, while the revengeful Francis bashed him over the head with a pillow.

At this point, the watchers relaxed; so did an exhausted Falstaff, who sat in the rocker with Doll on his knee, now surrounded by onstage voyeurs. Hal and Poins hid under the bedsheets before popping up to reveal themselves, at which Falstaff rose and unceremoniously dumped Doll on the floor. The lines Hands had used to indicate Falstaff's prurience at thrusting Doll on to Hal became a particularly pointed instance of treating her as sexual property. Responding to what she thought was a compliment ('honest, virtuous, civil gentlewoman' [II.iv.305-6]), Doll came on to Hal, who had joined her on the bed; and Falstaff's 'His grace says that which his flesh rebels against' (II.iv.354) became a double warning – 'Stay away, she's mine; she's not for you.' After a pause, Hal rose and handed Doll over to his 'father'. But this sudden antagonism, charged by Hal's self-disgust, quickly dissipated. Hal hugged Falstaff before he left, and Falstaff's own tearful goodbyes left Doll and Quickly wiping their eyes – like *Part One*'s Lady Percy and Lady Mortimer, similarly abandoned for more masculine business (III.i). Then, in a brilliant volte-face, Bardolph returned to announce that 'Falstaff is coming to Mistress Tearsheet.' Beaming mischievously, Falstaff plumped himself on the bed, unhooked his suspenders, and Doll threw herself on top of him. And the stage lights, as though eagerly complicit with Nunn's 'reward' to Falstaff for having been 'the observed of all observers', went to black in a fade reminiscent of old movies.

Such 'Hogarthian activity' did not appeal to all. Although most reviewers noted Nunn's 'remarkable talent for thickly populated, energetically sustained stage life' (*Times Literary Supplement*, 25

June 1982), some objected to the production's slow pace as well as to its obsessive, 'over-finicky' detail which, according to Michael Billington, '[lost] something of the physical momentum and medieval clarity of these extraordinary works' (*Guardian*, 10 June 1982). Billington's point of comparison was Hands's *Henrys*, which he had praised for their clarity and emblematic sweep and for evoking echoes of the plays' roots in the morality tradition. On one level, his remarks simply indicate a preference for Hands's production; but on another, he presupposes a stable register of meaning that a production *ought* to make available. His comments raise several issues. What would Hands's *Henrys* (or a production even more closely attuned to the plays' morality features) look like in 1982? What is the survival life of a particular production? *Should* exemplary productions be revived? Citing his own decision to revive Clifford Williams's *The Comedy of Errors* after ten years, Nunn assessed the contradictions posed by such a policy for a company committed to repeated productions of the same plays:

> We could revive much more of our work than we do. We tend to think of our work ... in very much the way that journalists think of their work; I mean, it's something to be completed, shown to the public, screwed up and thrown away. We don't think of a production continuing to be meaningful for ten years. One part of the artistic conscience says that times have changed, society has changed, expression has changed: therefore the play must have changed. And another part says: but actually I don't think differently about it. (Berry, *On Directing Shakespeare*, p. 63)

However problematic it may be for RSC directors, revival is a relative term. In theatrical practice, each successive production of a play revives and/or revises traces of its predecessors. Nunn raided Hands's staging of Rumour; he reacted to but did not copy what Hands had done with Falstaff's sexual possessiveness of and Hal's response to Doll as well as to Falstaff in the tavern–brothel scene. But Nunn's *Henrys* were also a very different kind of 'total theatre' than Hands's, one that even more fully – and freely – appropriated Brecht's *gestalt*. To Brecht, Shakespeare was a writer of emerging bourgeois individualism whose plays dramatised the clashes of value between feudal and capitalist economies. Foregrounding those contradictions was essential, in Brecht's view, to a modern staging, which should also heighten the spectators' awareness of the differences between their historical circumstances and those of the play's characters, not their insistent similarity. By using onstage observers to focus spectators' double awareness, especially in terms of class-based distinctions, Nunn embraced Brechtian alienation strategies wholeheartedly. And where Hands's tavern–brothel, with its scrims and single chair, had relied on Brecht's dictum of spare simplicity, Nunn's fully furnished chamber called particular attention to material objects and their accumulation, evoking to excess Brecht's insistence that stage properties be recognisably 'real'. Of the two, Nunn's production negotiated more obviously between past and present, then and now. On the one hand, its choices of *mise-en-scène* made historical difference a distinctly sensuous pleasure; on the other, Nunn's staging drew on pleasures which were recognisably those of present-day popular entertainments. In the tavern–brothel scene, for instance, Pistol's rooftop chase as well as the final blackout were cinematic borrowings; so was the production's musical score, in which motifs associated with particular characters made cross-references similar to those made possible by a film's sound track. If one (largely unvoiced) Company priority was indeed to resituate Shakespeare as a more marketable commodity, that also clearly contributed to Nunn's reassessment of the *Henrys*. And if the production's Brechtian strategies happened to foreground contradictory and relative aspects of the characters and their actions, what was perhaps equally obvious was that Nunn – and his actors – were having fun.

So did the reviewers. For in spite of whatever objections they made to Nunn's highly detailed *mise-en-scène*, they obviously enjoyed it: for most, the tavern–brothel scene, with what Irving Wardle called its 'goldmine of small performances', was *2 Henry IV*'s central attraction (*Times*, 10 June 1982). Certainly, too, Nunn's use of realistic stage spectacle could be justified in terms of the play, which slips easily and frequently into Shakespeare's particular brand of realism, especially in the tavern–brothel and Gloucestershire scenes. Intriguingly, reviewers objected less to the production's realism than to Rumour – 'a gratuitous spasm of theatricality that distract[ed] spectators from the continuity of political argument,' said the *Times Literary Supplement* (25 June 1982) – or to Nunn's decision to turn kingship itself into a public theatrical display. Once again, an insistence on 'textual purity' lies behind this aversion to the RSC's new commitment to spectacle. And after all, for two decades the RSC itself had been at least partly responsible for retraining spectators to admire productions in which 'Shakespeare' (supposedly) spoke for himself on a (relatively) bare stage. But these preconceptions and expectations also betray a misunderstanding of Nunn's use of theatrical spectacle to distinguish between Hal's competing fathers. In the case of Falstaff, spectacle deliberately pulled spectators into the pleasures of realistic representation; in the case of Henry IV, his identity was at times entirely absorbed by (extra-textual) ceremonial rituals. By situating each at the centre of a very different realm of theatrical spectacle, Nunn's production stressed Falstaff's *person* and Henry IV's *persona*.

An even broader cultural context bears directly on understanding Nunn's choices. Whether in the 1590s or the 1980s, royal display serves power's cause by managing dissent and inviting consent for a society's dominant ideologies, including the myth of kingship. One could argue, of course, that Shakespeare's texts never surround Henry IV's figure with the full social and ceremonial trappings of theatrical kingship: these are reserved for Henry V. Indeed, that distinction seems not only deliberate but deliberately political, for it highlights Henry IV's position as an illegitimate monarch who has usurped the throne and shores up Hal/Henry V's status as an ideal king. Yet these were the very points made by Nunn's staging. In *Part One*'s opening procession, for instance, the King appeared as an icon, surrounded by chanting monks. In much the same way that celebrations surrounding the United States' 'victory' in the 1991 Gulf War served to consolidate George Bush's power and to expiate memories of Vietnam, this public rite seemed designed to exorcise the King's guilt as well as that of the entire society. And at the close of *Part One*, Nunn's staging also went beyond the play's scripted limits to view Shrewsbury's victory through the King's eyes. Bare to the waist and wearing a large crucifix, Henry knelt in a tunnel of light, a shadowy kingdom of men and women standing in darkness behind him, witness to his solitary, agonised shame. By making Henry the object of his spectator–subjects' gaze, Nunn's staging enhanced his vulnerability to figure not royal power, but its lack. Although it is Falstaff who, at *Part One*'s close, promises reform, in Nunn's production it was the king who performed a Shrewsbury penance (Hodgdon 1991, p. 163). Both occasions, then, staged the sins of one particular father as a pageant of atonement for the eyes of offstage as well as onstage viewers, trapping his figure between them.

For the first time during the two plays, the King's initial appearance in *2 Henry IV* found him alone. Following the quick blackout on Falstaff's liaison with Doll, the lights came up to discover Henry IV seated at a writing table in a sparsely furnished private chamber that, aside from the *prie-dieu* in its corner, was an Elizabethan version of a present-day executive's office. Although the *Morning Star*'s reporter missed the aristocratic 'atmosphere of power and luxury which the same company brought to *Richard II*' (17 June 1982), that lack was, once again, precisely the point. Everything about the space, and the man within it, was rigidly ordered, pristinely clean; he wore a close-fitting Ghandi-like white tunic, buttoned to the chin. Without the public spectacle previously associated with his figure, he seemed reduced in scale: a straight-backed, tightly reined-in man who had deliberately isolated himself from others. As elsewhere, watchers observed his meditations, belying his assumption that his 'poorest subjects / Are at this hour asleep' (III.i.4-5). Although he stopped work during the soliloquy, after which he crossed to sit in the darkest corner of the chamber, as though to escape the watchers' eyes, he continued to shuffle papers and read letters once Warwick and Surrey entered. Dismissing their reassurances, he only grudgingly accepted their counsel, as though determined to bear the kingdom's cares alone. As in other productions, the interval followed this scene. Tolling bells and the *Adoramus te* heard at *Part One*'s processional assembly were heard over the King's final lines about the Holy Land, recalling his earlier, more publicly theatrical expressions of grief. Yet, although Nunn's *2 Henry IV* followed tradition in making the interval break remind spectators of the King's – and the kingdom's – disease, this scene, and Patrick Stewart's remote King Henry, were so overwhelmed by the rampant energies of the tavern–brothel that my own *memory* of the production relocated the interval after Nunn's carefully choreographed blackout on Falstaff's nightly revels (II.iv), not the king's sleeplessness.

If this instance of one spectator's selective memory – which plays a more important role in perception than is commonly understood – attests to anything, it suggests that the tavern–brothel's carnivalesque was an impossibly tough act (even for a king) to follow. Beyond that, it certainly aligns my viewing politics with those of Ackland's Falstaff, whose 'Give me *life* ... and there's an end' (*1 Henry IV*, V.iii.59-61) at Shrewsbury served as an epigraph for his entire performance. But the two juxtaposed scenes also provide a good introduction to one of the most intriguing features of Nunn's *Henrys*. Although Nunn coded the difference between

Henry IV and Falstaff in terms of theatrical spectacle, what was especially striking were the likenesses between Hal's two fathers, in that they represented opposite sides of the same coin.

This similarity went deeper than the familiar critical oppositions between holiday and everyday, carnival and rule, timelessness and time which separate tavern from court, clown from king. Just as the asceticism and inhibition of Stewart's Henry IV were coded by his costume, that of Ackland's Falstaff revealed his ostentation. Epaulettes adorned his leather jerkin, which bore the royal devices of lions and fleurs-de-lys in scarlet, blue and gold as showy signs of his Shrewsbury 'honors'. Like the returning veteran who feels his country owes him a debt, he demanded recognition and acclaim, and when that was denied him – whether by a tailor or a Chief Justice – he became resentful and aggressive. When the Chief Justice taunted him about being separated from Hal, Falstaff reacted by shaking his stick right in the grave Justice's face ('Yea; I thank your pretty sweet wit for it' [I.ii.207]). Yet before he left the stage, he put a penny in the alms box, as though to propitiate the gods of pox and gout. When the Chief Justice made it patently clear that neither he nor an embarrassed Gower wanted anything to do with Falstaff, his dismissive attitude fed the old knight's antagonism, already fuelled by his irritation with Mistress Quickly for attempting to take advantage of his new status (II.i). He heard the Chief Justice's 'thou art a great fool' (II.i.197-8) just before his exit; it stopped him in his tracks, and his shoulders sagged.

Stewart's Henry IV also felt that others underrated him and showed a similar concern for how 'history' had (and would) report him. If Falstaff's mercurial temper made others uncomfortable, the king made his courtiers uneasy and edgy: impatient with their attentiveness, he often turned on them abruptly, as though suspecting them of flattery or questioning their right to speak. Where Falstaff had what one critic called 'an unrefusable – even ferocious – amicability that would make any pub seem like home' (*Times Literary Supplement*, 25 June 1982) and loved to stage himself expansively for both his onstage and offstage audiences, Henry IV submerged his identity in official routine, spoke quietly, moved with great economy and sought isolation. Both Stewart and Ackland were recognisably ambitious, self-made men; both had impossible desires: for Henry IV, to make a penitential journey to the Holy Land; for Falstaff, to have 'the laws of England at [his] commandment' (V.iii.135-6). Both feared death. The news of

Glendower's death prompted Henry's collapse (III.i); several scenes later, when Prince John condemned Coleville, Falstaff reeled with shock (IV.ii). Each also desired a son he could not have. When Hotspur, arguing for his right to his prisoners, pulled a chair close to Henry IV's council table, at one point Henry reached out to touch him but then drew back his hand, pretending that he had intended only to sip from the small, highly polished goblet which was always present in his chambers (*1 Henry IV*, I.iii). And when, perched (most ironically) on a Brechtian cart of war, Falstaff spoke in praise of sack, the pause Ackland took after 'If I had a thousand sons ...' (*2 Henry IV*, IV.ii.118) came as a surprisingly poignant reminder that he had no son – not even Hal.

Calling attention to the traits Henry IV and Falstaff shared had distinct implications for the crown scene – traditionally the point at which Hal's rehearsals for royal identity become transformed into a 'true' performance – as well as its aftermath. Where previous Hals had contemplated the crown with awe or clearly desired it, Murphy's Hal was wary of it and addressed it angrily: it did indeed represent an enemy – the cause of his father's death and his own confusion. When he jammed the crown on his tangled curls, it obviously did not fit – the image was of a child playing dressing-up. As though feeling its weight, which intensified his sense of loss, he removed it from his head and left his father's side to sit, staring into space, on a bench in the shadows. Consequently, he missed seeing Henry turn in his sleep and reach out towards the crown (a detail Nunn may have borrowed from his 1976 *Romeo and Juliet*, where, just as Romeo drank the poison, Juliet's arm, which was twined about his neck, moved). Later, when Warwick told the King that Hal had been discovered weeping over the crown, Henry responded with a brittle laugh. At Hal's return, Henry's 'leave us here alone' (IV.iii.118-19) marked a look between father and son; once the others had left, the King abruptly held out his hand for the crown, and when Hal responded too slowly, Henry snatched it back. His accusations were bitter and violently sarcastic, and he turned his face away during Hal's apology, his emotion masked by his clenched jaw and tight mouth until, at 'O my son' (IV.iii.306), he finally reached out to embrace Hal. His touch unleashed Hal's grief: sobs wracked his trembling body, and he could hardly speak through the tears. Only because the crown catalysed this rush of feeling was the scene about legitimating its transfer; that was eclipsed by the sense that this represented a rare moment in an otherwise painful, tense father–son relationship where each could show his love for the other and where Murphy's Hal, without fear of reprimand, could reveal that he was still a child. Stunned by his father's approaching death, he lost the opportunity to redeem himself fully in the King's eyes; he heard the King's last advice as from a distance, and the promises he made were more to please the dying man than to assume his office. Where previous crown scenes had not only healed the fracture between father and son but marked Hal's commitment to the crown, Nunn's scene reached a much more hesitant, contradictory resolution. The two reviewers who did mention it called it the climax of the *play* – an assumption based more on their past viewing experience than on the evidence offered by Nunn's production.

Perhaps the most significant implication of Stewart's and Murphy's complex, ambiguous playing was that Hal's inability to cope with anything except his father's death delayed his coming of age as a monarch. And this, in turn, was coloured by the similarities between Henry IV and Falstaff. On the one hand, Hal had clearly made an emotional commitment to his 'true' father – a choice that implies Faltaff's 'death'; on the other, since any decision about Hal's behaviour as a future ruler remained open, it was entirely possible to believe that Hal still might choose to incorporate Falstaff within his new government. Furthermore, Ackland's Falstaff seemed a more probable (if still suspect) candidate for such a post than any before him. According to Benedict Nightingale, 'Falstaff's boast when he hears of the king's death ... sounds as formidable as triumphant in Mr. Ackland's mouth; and he makes us feel ... that he would command [the laws of England] for good as well as ill' (*New Statesman*, 18 October 1982). In short, Nunn's socio-psychological exploration of Shakespeare's text produced dramatic uncertainty that threw considerable weight forward on the accession scene as well as the rejection.

Nunn's staging of the accession scene suspended and delayed such issues further by making deliberate distinctions between Hal's family relationships and that with his new father, the Lord Chief Justice. At first, he sat hesitantly on the throne but rose to reassure his brothers (he hugged Gloucester and Clarence, but not John) before returning to it to put the Chief Justice on trial. Later, he crossed to kneel at the *prie-dieu* ('And princes all, ... I beseech you ... [V.ii.121]) and, with everyone kneeling behind him, offered a prayer to his father's memory. Because it looked more like what

Henry IV would have done than a gesture that came naturally to Hal, it was very much a performance. Yet this prayer also led to a more public self-presentation. Rising from his knees, Hal stepped from the 'throne room', circled upstage, and then, standing at centre-stage, delivered the last section of his set speech ('Now call we our high court of Parliament ... 'God shorten Harry's happy life one day!" [V.ii.133]) as a policy statement. Breaking up the speech in this way had two effects. For one, Hal's words became the fulfilment of *Part One*'s 'I know you all' (I.ii.192-214); for another, the burst of music and sudden blaze of light that enclosed and isolated his figure registered how quickly he had assumed the theatrical trappings of kingship.

Like many of Shakespeare's end games, *2 Henry IV*'s narrative drives almost mechanistically toward an even more highly theatricalised last scene. In performance, it is essential to keep that mechanism going forward, for if a production hesitates or slows down, spectators begin to question its logic. Nunn's staging foregrounded the mechanism itself. At the end of the first Gloucestershire scene (V.i), Falstaff's exit overlapped with the Lord Chief Justice's entrance (they could have seen one another); similarly, as the processional exit following the accession scene left the stage, Falstaff entered from the opposite side. Quite obviously, this strategy enhanced a sense of simultaneity and of events unfolding rapidly – and without Falstaff's knowledge. With extreme economy, it also made the point that the Lord Chief Justice had, quite literally, replaced Falstaff. He – and the play – were running out of time.

At the close, the stage-trucks were arranged to frame a diagonal corridor between them. While the entire community of watchers assembled, rush-strewers prepared the way for the royal entry, Pistol held up a T-shirt emblazoned with '*Si fortuna me tormenta, spero contenta*' and chanted '*Obsque hoc nihil est*' as an aggressive football slogan – two anachronisms connecting Pistol's own anachronistic figure to present-day political and social demonstrations – and Falstaff hurriedly positioned himself directly in the procession's path. Preceded by a crucifix-bearer as well as by Gloucester, Clarence and Prince John and followed by the Lord Chief Justice, Bardolph and Poins, Henry V entered wearing the heavily embroidered ceremonial white cope Henry IV had worn in the opening of *1 Henry IV*, his face a blank, unreadable mask. Once the King stepped from the coronation procession to address Falstaff, he regained expressiveness: choking back a sob and straining to smile, he approached Falstaff ('When thou does hear I am as I have been, / Approach me, and thou shalt be as thou wast' [V.v.60-1]) but then drew back, perhaps afraid he might (as he had so many times before) hug the old man. After asking the Lord Chief Justice 'to see performed the tenor of my word' (V.v.71), he paused as though he might continue – a nicely placed reminder of how, after *Part One*'s impromptu tavern playlet had been interrupted, Falstaff had urged, 'Play out the play! I have much to say in the behalf of that Falstaff' (II.iv. 478-9). He stood alone for a moment before being enveloped by the crowd, and as the procession continued offstage, Poins, in a brand new short cloak, marched proudly at its tail end and looked back over his shoulder to flip Falstaff a smug, triumphant grin.

During Hal's sermonising, Ackland's Falstaff took the new King's words standing: he did not slump or stagger; there were no tears, no invitation to sympathise. Standing with Shallow, Pistol and Bardolph, he watched the exiting procession and, just as it left the stage, he laughed – in Robert Cushman's words, as though 'this were one more inexplicable practical joke' (*Observer*, 13 June 1982). It was the final sign of his similarity to Henry IV, who, when told that the chamber where he had first collapsed was called Jerusalem, had also laughed at history's ironic situational joke (IV.iii.363). Only when he was arrested and sent to the Fleet did Ackland's Falstaff crack, yet he followed the arresting officer offstage with dignity. In contrast, Pistol broke away and, brandishing his T-shirt as he shouted his final line, he had to be dragged off, leaving behind a troubled Chief Justice, totally at odds with Prince John's elation over the coming war. Then the stage cleared to make way for the returning procession, which filled the entire space with an image almost like that which opened *Part One*. There, candles had flickered and streamed in the darkness; here, the light was harsh and steady. And only one monk, carrying a cross, walked behind this new King who, like his father before him, seemed uneasy in majesty's garment and had become a smiling mechanism of authority, flanked by his subjects and official representatives but, unlike his father, as yet unaccompanied by any choral anthem of praise.

By figuring *2 Henry IV*'s close as a reprise of Henry IV's image of power in atonement, Nunn's staging represented succession as an instance of *plus ça change, plus c'est le même chose*. In its Folio configuration, however, *2 Henry IV* directs an exit for Prince John and the Lord Chief Justice, leaving an empty stage – a point Nunn had observed when he co-directed the *Henrys* with John Barton and Clifford Williams in 1966 and one which realises the double absences of both king and clown. In 1982, Nunn turned that emptiness into a panoptical view of authority: aristocracy and the populace united in one processional image to represent 'England'. Such an image, connecting theatrical history – especially the traditions of Victorian stage spectacle – to national history and attaching a final panoply of unity to the play, comfortably and reassuringly suited the RSC's anniversary occasion and the Barbican opening. It also, however, suggested the ideological contradictions masked by this image of containment. For there was little sense, as Nunn's *2 Henry IV* ended, that Henry V had accepted kingship; instead, he seemed to be inhabiting its robes only for the purposes of the coronation ceremony. However strong the appeal of this final spectacle, it was hard to forget that it had been achieved at the expense of the richly-detailed sense of life characteristic of this production, which, at the close, hollowed out one mode of theatrical representation and replaced it with another. To the extent that such foreclosure exposes authority itself as empty theatrical celebration, Nunn's processional close was the perfect epilogue for a production which had exposed power itself as suspect, subject to telling itself lies as well as to the rumours and (mis)interpretations of its subjects (see Hodgdon 1991, pp. 177-8).

By relying on spectacle as a means of interrogating past (and present) social history, Nunn's *Henrys* marked a shift in the plays' cultural capital. It would be difficult to reconstruct precisely the socio-historical circumstances that made so many reviewers willing to envision Falstaff as a potential lawmaker. But one fact seemed certain. By including *Merry Wives*, Hands's 1975 centenary season had approximated a 'Falstaff cycle', but Nunn's productions had come closer to what some had called Shakespeare's plays in his own lifetime, *Falstaff, Parts One* and *Two*. What was equally interesting was that not a single reviewer mentioned the loss of *Henry V* from what had become accepted as a cycle, whether a tetralogy or a trilogy. It was certainly clear from Murphy's Hal that an heroic future for the character lay well beyond *2 Henry IV*'s scripted limits. But no reviewer desired to see a sequel. Was it that no one wanted to imagine the kind of monarch this Hal might have made?

I Stratford-upon-Avon, 1951; Richard Burton as Prince Hal, Harry Andrews as Henry IV. Shakespeare Centre Library; photo: the estate of Angus McBean

II Stratford-upon-Avon, 1951; Richard Burton as Henry V, Anthony Quayle as Falstaff. Shakespeare Centre Library; photo: the estate of Angus McBean

III Stratford-upon-Avon, 1975; Sydney Bromley as Shallow; Trevor Peacock as Silence. Mig Holte Photographic Collection, the Shakespeare Centre Library; photo: Mig Holte

IV Stratford-upon-Avon, 1975; Alan Howard as Henry V, Brewster Mason as Falstaff. Mig Holte Photographic Collection, Shakespeare Centre Library; photo: Mig Holte

V London, 1982; Gerard Murphy as Prince Hal, Patrick Stewart as Henry IV. Photo: Chris Davies

VI London, 1982; Gerard Murphy as Prince Hal, Joss Ackland as Falstaff. Photo: Chris Davies

VII English Shakespeare Company, 1986; June Watson as Mistress Quickly,
Jenny Quayle as Doll Tearsheet. Photo: Laurence Burns

VIII English Shakespeare Company, 1986; Michael Pennington as Henry V, Barry Stanton as Falstaff.
Photo: Laurence Burns

CHAPTER VI

Shakespeare in the age of electronic reproduction: Michael Bogdanov (1986-89)

I

Among the news cuttings for the Quayle–Redgrave 1951 Festival season is a Giles cartoon depicting the façade of the Shakespeare Memorial Theatre, where, in the foreground of a long queue, one noticeably *nouveau-riche* couple stand out. The woman, much larger than any other figure, including her cigar-toting husband, is saying, 'Listen, Elmer, we've got Bob Hope tomorrow, Danny Kaye Thursday – but it's going to be Bill Shake and Henry Four tonight. Now stop beefing.' Just ahead of her in the queue, nearly hidden among the others, stands the tiny figure of Shakespeare, a hand in his breeches pocket and a somewhat bemused look on his ruff-framed face (*Daily Express*, 9 May 1951). Aside from the joke of imagining Shakespeare as an unnoticed playgoer for productions that promised to honour his 'intentions', the cartoon marks off foreign from native entertainers and low- from high-culture entertainments. Linked to 'Henry Four', 'Bill Shake' remains firmly in place as a cultural icon; the Shakespeare Memorial Theatre author-ises both; and theatregoing is represented (and insisted upon by a woman) as a cultural duty.

Thirty-six years later and at another venue, Bill Shake's cultural authority had undergone a sea-change. At Toronto's Royal Alexandra Theatre, where Michael Bogdanov's *The Henrys* was playing but where a poster advertised *Sweet Charity*, a season ticket-holder offered to sell Bogdanov his tickets at half-price.

'What's on?' said Bogdanov. 'I don't know,' replied the man, *'Richard and Henry Get Laid ...'* (Bogdanov and Pennington, p. 90). Reduced to half-price, Shakespeare not only loses his commercial draw but, more importantly, is subsumed within 'the popular', where (at least in one spectator's view) he becomes inseparable from other, supposedly more viable, offerings.

Giles's cartoon and this anecdote do more than simply call attention to the shifting commercial status of performed Shakespeare – from Festival hot-ticket item to box-office reject. They also invite questions about Shakespeare productions aimed at particular venues and particular audiences; about their relative accessibility (or inaccessibility), including their cost; and about whether 'Shakespeare' is still present – not just standing in the queue but recognisably 'embodied' within the staged representation which bears his name. These issues are hardly new, nor do they pertain exclusively to Shakespeare; rather, they circulate within the wider context of a complex, variable, relentlessly faddish entertainment market-place economy. And it is not only Shakespeare whose theatrical future (as Trevor Nunn had noted in the late 1970s; see Chapter V) is in jeopardy. In late twentieth-century Britain, for example, only 6 per cent of the population go to the theatre at all; even fewer attend opera or ballet performances (Bogdanov and Pennington, p. 235). Yet despite such hazardous circumstances, Shakespeare retains considerable power and commands attention in popular as well as high-culture spheres. Even commercial Hollywood dubs him 'Billy Big Boy'; and in 1985 Britain, as Michael Bogdanov and Michael Pennington discovered, his name opened up public as well as commercial coffers to support the English Shakespeare Company, formed around a firm commitment to tour up-market, large-scale Shakespeare throughout the United Kingdom and overseas.

Brought together by shared dissatisfactions with the 'snafus and treacheries' of the British repertory system, Bogdanov and Pennington felt the need to be independent of the big theatrical institutions, the National Theatre and the RSC, where both had worked – Bogdanov as a director, Pennington as an actor. They themselves have documented the first three years of the ESC's history, during which the Company first mounted *The Henrys* and then expanded their offerings to include *Richard II*, the *Henry VI* plays and *Richard III* as a seven-play cycle, *The Wars of the Roses*. A brief summary of the sponsorship arrangements for and the extent of their tour – what Pennington would later call 'an unfashionable cultural service' – will give some idea of the scope of their enterprise. Initial funding for *The Henrys* came from public and private sources: £100,000 from the Arts Council; £125,000 from the Canadian entrepreneurial team of Ed and David Mirvish, owners of London's Old Vic Theatre, who stipulated that the Company would play both at the Old Vic and at the Royal Alexandra in Toronto; and £65,000 from the Allied Irish Bank (in their first major arts sponsorship), an amount that was recognised by £25,000 from the government's Business Sponsorship Scheme, administered by the Association for Business Sponsorship of the Arts. However much the Arts Council supported a policy of devolution from London, since its charter prevents it from funding work outside the United Kingdom, it contributed just 38 per cent of the ESC's three-year production costs (and nothing to running costs), while the remaining 62 per cent of their funding came from commercial sources. The ESC's thirty-three-week UK tour included Plymouth, Cardiff, Glasgow, Liverpool, Southampton, Norwich, Nottingham, Bath, Hull, Sunderland, Leeds, Oxford, Manchester and Birmingham; eventually, *Wars* was seen not only in Canada but in the United States (Chicago and Stamford, Connecticut), in Tokyo (where it opened the Tokyo Globe), Berlin, Paris, Australia, Hong Kong and Holland before returning to play at the York Festival, at the Old Vic and at Swansea's Grand Theatre (where it was televised) before closing in early 1989. (Bogdanov and Pennington, pp. 4-7, 235-6; *London Standard*, 17 September 1986). Although the ESC certainly fared better than touring theatrical troupes in Shakespeare's day – who received only 5s per week when in the country, as opposed to 10s in London (see Bentley, pp. 177-9, 183-90, 205, 240 for particulars of Elizabethan touring companies) – what was especially ironic about the tangled history of securing financial capital to stage plays often designated as a national epic was that commercial funding, together with receipts from overseas touring, enabled the Company to bring *The Henrys* and *Wars* to provincial British audiences. And as it turned out, what gave the ESC's financial history an added ideological charge was that its major source of *cultural* capital came not from London critics, but from regional and overseas audiences and reviewers.

Of all the productions examined in this volume, the ESC's *Henrys* and the later *Wars of the Roses* stake out the most thoroughgoing claim for a popular Shakespeare. Although such a label may not necessarily imply a Shakespeare set apart from traditional or mainstream interpretive strategies, the ESC productions also succeeded in mapping out a distinctive theatrical territory and in offering up an alternative Shakespeare for the late 1980s. From the beginning, Bogdanov and Pennington insisted on separating their project from traditionally British production practices and styles. Recognising the need for authoritative casting throughout, they recruited a minimal acting company of twenty-five who would stretch to cover all the roles: 'double, treble, turn themselves inside out, and move the furniture'. As Pennington put it, 'The feel of our enterprise (and our salaries) would have to be attractive enough to tempt the middleweights we needed; and we would also need the right young actors from repertory, out of town and fringe, with a certain flair and fearlessness and an unaffected air: street credibility, in fact. The whole trick would be in the mix' (Bogdanov and Pennington, p. 17). Not only were they convinced that such a practical, and rarely experienced, sense of ensemble was crucial to communicating with the audiences they wished to reach, but they were also determined to encourage actors to use their natural regional accents. 'Nothing', claimed Pennington, 'is more deadly than to hear someone struggling for a received accent because it's Shakespeare and posh; nothing could be less like Shakespeare's theatre or our intentions; and since the plays echo and re-echo with the sounds of Bangor, Northumberland and Southwark, those actors should if possible come from there. Or close by' (Bogdanov and Pennington, pp. 17-18). Appalled by a recent RSC production at the Barbican, where 'the elaborate set was lit, but not the actors' faces' and where the production's 'rationalist tone' and the actors' 'elaborate gestures of illustration' generalised the text, Pennington had high hopes for making the ESC

> the best bloody verse-speaking outfit in the country. ... Our style of playing will be accurate and fastidious, in detail and stress, but it will come from urgent need. We will light the actors as da Vinci recommended and Gordon Craig echoed: from above and the side as you see them in life, lit by the sun. The set will make the imaginary forces work, and not show off. (Bogdanov and Pennington, p. 19)

Where RSC policy since Peter Hall's directorship had acknowledged the importance of 'relevance' by staging those plays that 'made some demand upon our critical attention' (Trevor Nunn, quoted in Berry, *On Directing Shakespeare*, p. 56), Bogdanov's commitment to relevance is keyed to his vision of theatre as an instrument of sociopolitical critique. Sounding much like Brecht, he insists that 'the only reason to make theatre is to initiate change' (Hodgdon interview). What made the *Henrys* especially appealing were the obvious parallels between the England of Henry Bolingbroke and that of Margaret Thatcher, in which Bogdanov saw Jan Kott's Grand Mechanism at work:

> [T]he escalator shuttling mice and men up to the top, where the golden crock of Imperialism shone brightly, waiting for the next attempt to snatch it from its podium. We were in the era of New Brutalism where a supposed return to Victorian values under the guise of initiative and incentive masked the true goal of greed, avarice, exploitation and self. Westminster Rule. Centralisation. Censorship. Power to the City. Bleed the rest of the country dry. ... Boardrooms may have replaced the Palace at Westminster, Chairpersons (mainly men) replaced monarchs, but the rules were the same. All of which added a spur to the *Henrys* project – provided the passion for portrayal. How could the plays *not* be understood in a contemporary context?' (Bogdanov and Pennington, pp. 24-5)

Emphasising the *Henrys*' sociopolitical topicality through Brechtian –Marxist lenses of materialist critique, it could be argued, offers a perspective at least as totalising – and as academically grounded – as Redgrave's Tillyardian neo-providentialism, Hands's notions of 'Shakespearean simplicity' or Nunn's encompassing social meta-narrative. Both Hands and Nunn, after all, had raided Brecht's aesthetic and incorporated features of his practice in their productions, making him serve both individual and Company visions of 'Elizabethanism'. But Bogdanov's theatrical politics embrace Brecht as Shakespeare's heir, linking the two through their shared attitudes to history. Neither, for example, is particularly interested in chronology, and the historical moments each dramatises are 'selective, typical, compressed, and real in the sense that all historicity is grounded in politics, religion, popular myths and the class struggle' (Kowsar, p. 470). After all, since Shakespeare's plays use past history to address issues current in the 1590s, Bogdanov could justify the ESC's practice as a continuation of that process. Put another way, if performed Shakespeare is to retain its signifying power in present-day culture, it must contain something more than mere expressiveness, images of medieval pageantry and royal protocol or reflexive meditations on Shakespeare's 'greatness'. Not only must it act as a vehicle for the spectator's consciousness, but it must reinvent itself (see Blau, esp. p. 457).

For Bogdanov, reinventing Shakespeare is synonymous with

making him accessible. He makes claims for a populist theatre that takes Shakespeare out of the hands of literary critics and restores him to present-day spectators – especially those who have been bored, baffled or mystified by an academic Bard, whether in schoolrooms or in theatres. Noting his own 'incomprehension when presented with obscure, effete, literary productions hailed by the critics as "masterly re-evaluations"', Bogdanov aims 'at giving audiences some kind of folk memory as to what the stories are, so that they can be handed down'. Moreover, he speaks of 'releasing' and clarifying the language in order to 'open the plays out for new, young audiences' who may not have read or seen the plays and who have spare knowledge of English history. 'Unless I assume this,' Bogdanov writes, 'I am being elitist, joining that group who would ignore popular methods of communication, denying that the plays were performed for a whole cross-section of the community, some educated, some not' (Bogdanov, quoted in Berry, *On Directing Shakespeare*, p. 219; Bogdanov and Pennington, pp. 26, 43). In theatrical terms, that meant putting the plays in modern dress – a hallmark of Bogdanov's productions which reviewers, depending on the degree of their attachment to familiar traditions of representation, had often found either unilluminating or at cross-purposes with 'Shakespeare's intentions'.

Considering how difficult it is to discern the intentions of living playwrights, Bogdanov finds the idea of reproducing Shakespeare's intentions suspect, a matter that has more to do with obeying theatrical convention than with certain knowledge. Yet although he has consistently defended his choice of modern dress for Shakespeare as one way to make the plays more available, he quickly realised that 'total modern dress for the *Henrys* was out', primarily because the Hal–Hotspur fight had to be a medieval combat. Recalling Henry Peacham's famous drawing (*c*. 1595) of a scene from *Titus Andronicus*, which shows some figures wearing an approximation of Roman togas and others dressed as Elizabethan soldiers, Bogdanov found his solution in Shakespeare's own theatrical practice. Much as Hands had let *Henry V*'s opening Chorus dictate his production's design, Bogdanov took direction from this 'eclectic theatre of expediency':

> We would provide a space that would allow the plays to range over the centuries in imagery. We would free our, and the audiences', imaginations by allowing an eclectic mix of costumes and props, choosing a time and a place that was most appropriate for a character or a scene.

Modern dress at one moment, medieval, Victorian or Elizabethan the next. We would use a kit of props ... [which], as far as possible, would remain on stage. The means of transformation from one scene to the next would remain visible. No tricks up our sleeves (until we needed one). We would create a style that was essentially rough theatre, but would add, when we needed it, a degree of sophistication. It was stick and cloth brought up to date ... the whole budget for props and furniture was only £10,000. (Bogdanov and Pennington, pp. 28-9)

These decisions reflect specific borrowings from Brecht *à la* Peter Brook (with whom Bogdanov had worked on the famous 1971 *Dream*), especially the idea of 'no tricks' and the set, both of which call attention to the non-illusionistic nature of the theatrical event. Chris Dyer's set design – a black steel structure backed by an upstage projection screen mounted on a steel framework and equipped with large, sliding centre doors – evoked the age of mechanical reproduction; at stage-left and right, two moveable scaffold-like towers flanked a central bridge, which could be raised or lowered to operate on several levels. The mechanics of flying, the lighting bridge and the surrounding stage walls were all visible, evidence of Bogdanov's 'raw approach', his desire to 'strip away meaningless design clichés' to create 'a theatre within a theatre' (Bogdanov and Pennington, p. 29). In surrounding the *Henrys* with machine-modern trappings, Dyer's set provided a space for staging history as something other than a pictorial discourse designed to commemorate, and contain, a lost Elizabethan past.

Bogdanov's costume designer, Stephanie Howard, also worked to escape the associations of a specific period, rejecting the visual and conceptual unity reminiscent of late nineteenth-century practice for a radically disassociative mix of styles. Remarking that 'an eclectic style in form-obsessed English theatre is (or was then) a novelty', Bogdanov contrasts European practice, where eclecticism is the norm and where content and argument 'released by a series of conflicting images, idea joggers, memory aids, etc' are more important than purity of concept (Bogdanov and Pennington, p. 30). Here again, he assumes that removing a Shakespeare play from the conservative (or even reactionary) sociopolitical or cultural context created by traditional aesthetics opens up the possibility of critique. Importantly, however, what remained in place were markers designating a character's social status and rank. Bogdanov sketches out some of the design solutions:

[Howard] quickly identified the pure design areas – the women, the Court – and decided that areas like the Boar's Head [and] the street ...

were bag and rag. It is Stephanie who can claim credit for the punk Mohican hairstyle of Gadshill ..., an image that became something of a symbol for the ESC style. Unfairly, as it happens, because although the final blend was the result of a scramble to find ... anything that could possibly be used, the essential concept was carefully thought through, and costumes selected for period and feel according to the character and the scene. ... [T]he basic concept is *theatrical*, [and] lies in the careful blending and selecting. ... We needed a splash of colour. The Court would have a set of red and blue uniforms, a Royal tunic that vaguely stretches back to the beginning of the nineteenth century, and that, to this day, is worn for ceremonial occasions. Frock coats would complete the political Westminster look, an image that is not so long gone ... . There would be some cloaks for the Coronation Scene. ... Rebels would be guerrillas in berets, jeans, combat jackets, fatigues. Street and tavern would be modern, Elizabethan (drawers), some fifties, some thirties. Pistol – a Rocker.... (Bogdanov and Pennington, pp. 31-2)

Where Nunn had given the *Henrys* 'relevance' by framing them within a city meta-narrative, Bogdanov's eclecticism makes a similar move to place the plays within a referential network that embraces the spectators' world. 'Looking back at now' was Elaine Williams's apt phrase (*Times Educational Supplement*, 24 June 1988) for a style which drew mixed critical response, especially from those for whom a particular mode of theatrical representation is essential to retelling 'Shakespeare-history'. Speaking for the traditionalists, Giles Gordon remarked that the 'crucial hierarchical distinctions of early fifteenth-century England go for nothing, and a fundamental aspect of the play is lost' (*London Daily News*, 23 March 1987). *Punch*'s Robin Ray, on the other hand, found the experience distinctly pleasurable:

Bogdanov has concocted his production ... much as a berserk chef might whip up a stir-fry .... Chop the text, and fillet, add strips of dialogue to taste, flavour with a bouquet garni of accents and gags plus a liberal sprinkling of stage business. Peel any costumes to hand, mixing armour with battle-dress, frock-coats with leather and punk, and blend with automatic firearms side-by-side-by-broadswords. Marinate harps, electric guitars, trombone, flute and synthesisers with music from Handel to 'The Ball of Kerrymuir', add microphones drenched in echo; simmer for six hours. It tastes funny, but the audience lapped it up, and so did I. The letter may have been disregarded, but the spirit remains intact. (8 April 1987)

The difference between 'letter' and 'spirit' points to the perceived threat that making Shakespeare our contemporary will not only erase the 'crucial hierarchical distinctions' of which Gordon speaks but dismantle past interpretive traditions altogether. Situating the

ESC's style within the cultural dominant of postmodernism – what Fredric Jameson calls 'the cultural logic of late capitalism' – will help to contextualise that issue (Jameson, 'Postmodernism').

Put in theoretical terms, the postmodern is characterised by depthlessness, a waning of historicity and the random cannibalisation of signs stored in global memory, all of which work to erase specific temporality and deny the pastness of the past. Tied to a popular appetite for seeing the world transformed into images of itself, into pseudo-events and pseudo-spectacles, these features construct a predominantly spatial logic which privileges not 'the real', but its surface appearances, from which original signifieds have been erased. In that the ESC productions construct a pastiche of the stereotypical past and present – what Ihab Hassan calls 'present-ification' (p. 91) – they do indeed risk recuperating history merely as 'a glossy finish', as style. But one can also argue that, by disrupting the theatrical codes which work to keep history at a safe distance, Bogdanov's *Henrys* invite spectators to experience history actively. By this logic, ESC style works to jolt spectators into recognising the connections as well as the distinctions between one era and another and, perhaps, alerting them to the need for present-day historical change. And, as Jameson writes, such recognitions ultimately reverse any ahistorical tendency and 're-store proper tension to the notion of historical – [and, I would add, social] – difference' (see Jameson, 'Postmodernism,' pp. 58, 65-6, 68, 75; and 'On Magic Realism', p. 303).

Bogdanov's postmodern collage clearly 'speaks Shakespeare' through a representational politics that differs from Redgrave's neo-Tillyardian world picture, Hands's 'pure Shakespeare' or Nunn's view of the *Henrys* as social history. Articulating those differences also returns to the questions of cultural property and ownership, accessibility, and the presence or absence of 'Shakespeare' raised by Giles's cartoon and Bogdanov's anecdote – issues that the ESC productions bring into particularly sharp focus. As Pierre Bourdieu observes, 'The 'eye' is a product of history reproduced by education' (*Distinction*, p. 3). In the case of Shakespeare, such an 'educated' vision often seems committed to preserving his plays within a realm of high culture where 'classic theatre' retains the illusion that it is politically blind. To speak, as Thomas Clayton does, of the 'Bogdanovation' of Shakespeare and of his 'systematic didacticism' is both to ignore Tillyard's equally didactic politics and to reaffirm them as more 'Shakespearian' (pp. 229, 234). Yet the ESC's enthusiastic audiences in conservative provincial cities, as well as abroad, indicated a ready acceptance for an avowedly Marxist, 'mass culture' Shakespeare.

Several further observations are of particular interest here. Since theatre is not cheap in later-day capitalism, more than one critic remarked that those for whom Bogdanov intended his postmodernist collage might not easily afford a ticket, either to individual plays or for the eventual cycle presentations. That reviews of Redgrave's, Hands's and Nunn's productions do not mention ticket prices suggests that they were aimed at audiences for whom economic considerations, and the class distinctions they reassert, were erased by Shakespeare's larger cultural authority. Of the four, the ESC productions remain most consistently alert to the politics of theatre as, most likely, the Elizabethans knew them. For, just as the social and material conditions of Shakespeare's theatre blurred distinctions between kings and clowns and between high and low art, endowing the popular with a new seriousness which recuperated the historical past as the present and, through anachronism and insistent topicality, made chronology invisible, so too do the ESC's postmodernist representational strategies extend Shakespeare's *Henrys* beyond both their originating circumstances and the bounds of their currently authoritative cultural ownership. And accepting or challenging such ownership turns on how each staging of Shakespeare's history participates in a particular fashion of Elizabethanism. On the one hand, the productions of Redgrave, Hands and Nunn are specifically English theatrical commodities which reflect the insular xenophobia characterising the later years of Elizabeth's reign. On the other, the ESC productions reach beyond such local cultural signs to situate England, and English history, within the discourses of an international media community. In both cases, however, what seems clear is that the late 1590s and the late 1980s share similar anxieties about national and international identities and are similarly concerned with negotiating the cultural tensions between them.

II

First, a word about evidence. Unlike other stagings described in this volume, the ESC productions had a complex evolutionary history. 'Theatre for me, now, is always work in progress', said Bogdanov of the Company's three-year-long project (Bogdanov and

Pennington, p. 59). Although fundamental concepts remained the same in the move from *The Henrys* to *Wars* and from one touring venue to another over those years, some scenes were restaged in order to clarify their dynamics. Major casting changes also occurred. Over the years, there were two Hals (Michael Pennington and John Dougall), two Falstaffs (John Woodvine and Barry Stanton), three Henry IVs (Patrick O'Connell, John Castle and Michael Cronin), three Pistols (John Price, John Castle and Paul Brennan) and three Dolls (Jenny Quayle, Lynette Davies and Francesca Ryan). While some performers were content to step into the role as created by a predecessor and make it their own, others totally refashioned previous characterisations, which affected stage business as well as costume (For a partial record of these changes, see Bogdanov and Pennington, *passim*). Furthermore, in addition to the doubling required by the small ensemble, individual performances featured unexpected doubles. In Toronto, for example, Pennington played Wart on at least one occasion, setting up surprising resonances between the crippled, raggedy figure who collapsed in terror as Shallow's caliver went off (III.ii) and the steel-cold Henry V, delivering 'Once more unto the breach' (*Henry V*, III.i.1-34) from the top of a tank. What follows, then, draws primarily on performances of *The Henrys* (Toronto) and of *Wars* (Chicago) but includes some detail from the television production.

Asked how he saw the ESC's work as different from that offered by the other major theatrical institutions, Bogdanov replied,

> I'm trying to give the public a company that knows, every time it's on stage, what it's doing, what it's saying, why it's there, how every single character and every single line fits into social and political structures. ... The Company is all travelling in the same direction: it knows where it's heading with the story and the social structure of the plot. (Berry, *On Directing Shakespeare*, 224)

What Bogdanov says sounds much like the RSC's overall policy, one aimed at clarity and understanding. Enclosed within two cycle frameworks – *The Henrys* and *The Wars of the Roses* – *2 Henry IV* certainly pointed, as did Redgrave's and Hands's productions, towards *Henry V*. From the outset, however, the ESC mapped out a somewhat different route for Hal's emergence as England's new ruler. For one thing, Bogdanov's view of the histories as 'the ultimate English soap opera' – 'Experience lust, greed, deceit, murder and revenge all in one fun-filled weekend', read a Chicago newspaper's ad for *Wars* – led him to blur the limits of each play in order to provide a 'hook' for the sequel. Although 'to be continued' is a notion common to all cycle presentations, making *Part One*'s ending more open and unresolved had distinct implications for *Part Two* – a play Bogdanov believes should properly be called *Falstaff*.

Only once in *1 Henry IV* do King Henry and Falstaff share the stage. When, at the parley before Shrewsbury, the King asks Worcester how he came to rebel, Falstaff answers for him, 'Rebellion lay in his way, and he found it', and Hal quickly silences him ('Peace, chewet, peace!' [V.i.28-9]). Although Falstaff does not speak again until Henry IV has left the stage, both Hands's and Nunn's productions took this opportunity to sketch in their rivalry. In Hands's staging, both the King and Falstaff started to leave, and when Falstaff turned back to plead with Hal ('If thou seest me down in battle ...' [V.i.121]), Emrys James's Henry IV paused to watch them, as though to make sure that Hal would keep his promise to 'redeem all this on Percy's head' (III.ii.133) rather than revert to playing holiday with Falstaff. Patrick Stewart, Nunn's Henry IV, was caught between envy of and contempt for Falstaff: he turned away, his shoulders sagging in defeat as Hal joked with Falstaff. In an interview, Emrys James remarked, 'One can conceive a marvellous scene being written about [Henry and Falstaff] – a meeting between them' (Mullin, p. 31). Though it may not have been what James had in mind, Bogdanov's production did stage such a meeting – one borrowed from Orson Welles's *Chimes at Midnight*, which Bogdanov had seen as part of his preparation for *The Henrys* (Bogdanov and Pennington, p. 54).

Welles's film delays Falstaff's 'presentation' of Hotspur's corpse to Hal and his demands for recognition until after the rebels' sentencing and Henry's concluding remarks (*1 Henry IV*, V.iv-v). Rather than marking Hal's double reconciliation with his fathers, Shrewsbury's aftermath shows Hal deeply at odds with them both. As Falstaff dumps Hotspur's body on the ground, Hal kneels beside it; in a mid-long shot of Hal, a figure enters the frame at left, and the camera, rising with Hal, moves left to reveal the King, who faces his son, his back to the camera. A tightly edited sequence of close-ups – Henry's anguished face, Hal's look, Falstaff's glow of self-pleasure – links the three figures in an ambiguous web of doubt, betrayal and dishonour in which Falstaff's 'I look to be either earl or duke, I can assure you' (V.iv.139-40) cancels Hal's response. In a long shot, father and son face each other across

Hotspur's body before the King strides past Hal into the background where, mounting his horse, he collapses over the saddle. In the next sequence, a triumphant Falstaff, standing beside a huge wine keg and surrounded by his ragged soldiers, offers a tankard to Hal, who takes it and drinks, his forced smile a contrast to the others' laughter. As Falstaff's own smile disappears, Hal walks away across the smoke-filled battlescape, dropping the tankard in the dust; the soundtrack registers only the wind's empty roar, and the shot fades out. Economically, Welles's film sharply triangulates father–son oppositions to entrap a doubly-orphaned Hal between his rival fathers: cut off by one, he rejects the other. In eclipsing Falstaff's bulk with Hal's receding figure, Welles's film anticipates Sir John's ultimate rejection where he, not Hal, will disappear into the deep-space background of a long shot.

Deliberately quoting Welles's film – and acknowledging the debt with admiration – Bogdanov not only reordered the play's final events to set Hal apart from both fathers but, by linking Hal to Falstaff through Hotspur, brought out the contradictory nature of honour even more markedly than either *Chimes* or Shakespeare's play. At one point in the Hal–Hotspur fight, Hal lost his broadsword and, as though overcome with infantile fear, curled into a foetal position: with a grin, Hotspur slid the sword across to him, a chivalric gesture that cost him his life. Later, when Hal asked for leave to dispose of the prisoners, he was quite clearly playing 'chivalric son' for Henry IV, and it was at this point that Falstaff entered with Hotspur's body to claim his own honours ('I look to be either earl or duke ...' [V.iv.139-40]). Protesting that he had killed Hotspur, Hal was silenced by Falstaff's 'Lord, Lord, how this world is given to lying!' (V.iv.142-3) and, then, forced to step back by his father's outstretched sword. After a dismissive glance at his son, Henry turned on his heel and left. As Falstaff promised reform, Hal bent over Hotspur's body and took back the neckerchief he had worn in the earlier tavern scenes and had tied around the dead Hotspur's neck – a mark of his kill through which he reaccepted both his father's contempt and his rival's rebelliousness. Spoken with visceral disgust, Hal's 'bring your luggage *nobly* on your back ...' (V.iv.153) was shrugged off by Falstaff, who lifted Hotspur's body on to a cart piled with dead bodies and followed its slow circle offstage. Alone, Hal turned upstage and, raising his sword and Hotspur's over his head, exited after his father into the gathering dark, to the accompaniment of crashing brasses.

Like Welles's ending for Shrewsbury, Bogdanov's staging sharply focused Hal's exclusion through an exchange of looks that turned him back into an unredeemed son. Reversing the play's final incidents explained his estrangement from his father in *Part Two*, pointing his need to prove himself again to the King who, doubting his true son, had believed the boastful lie of another, counterfeit, father. For David Prosser, these moments marked Falstaff's rejection:

> Kingship, [Hal] sees in that moment, is going to be a continual process of gilding enormities with the happiest terms he has. It is in that moment that Hal accepts and understands his royal destiny, and it is in that moment that Falstaff is forsaken, as such a man must be. (*The Whig-Standard Magazine*, 30 May 1987)

Rejection, however, cut several ways. For Falstaff's actions also took revenge for Hal's exposure of his Gadshill cowardice by constructing a Shrewsbury joke not unlike Henry IV's 'shadows' marching in armour (see Hodgdon, 1991, pp. 163-6). And just as these moments called the limits of all counterfeiting into question, they also marked Hal and Falstaff as equally opportunistic subjects of a king who, with no less expediency, had helped to stage his own rise to power. Nobody, save perhaps Hotspur, left Shrewsbury's field with 'honour'. But the most overarching result of framing *2 Henry IV* between two rejections was that Falstaff's comic world – which, in Ray Conlogue's phrase, 'tends to bring on a severe case of Elizabethan fantasizing for most viewers' (*Globe and Mail*, 25 May 1987) – was revealed not as history's amusingly playful carnival alternative, but as its dangerous double.

In place of Rumour's prologue, the first evidence of *2 Henry IV*'s post-Shrewsbury kingdom was a visual image. At centre-stage stood a towering pile of guns, boards, shields, scrap metal, ladders and lengths of rope – left-over battle refuse. Amidst swirling smoke and in half-light, scavengers looted the rubbish pile as the cart of war, piled with bodies, circled the stage. Three sentries (in later stagings, the King, in a dressing gown, flanked by two uniformed officers) watched from the bridge. It was an especially apt image for the state of a nation where nothing was fastened down and everything was up for grabs. Exploitation had invaded honour's realm, shrinking and altering its signs. Although Hal wore the neckerchief he had taken from Hotspur's body throughout (and into *Henry V*), his Shrewsbury tabard, thrown over the back of a ratty couch in his apartments, had become an antimacassar (II.ii). Falstaff now wore Hotspur's black headband, which gave him the air of an ageing hippie (I.ii); and the trolley which had once borne the honourable dead became, with the addition of his favourite upholstered chair, a conveniently appointed phaeton that carried him to Gloucestershire and into 'battle' at Gaultree (III.ii; IV.ii). When a silver-armoured Coleville surrendered to him, Falstaff, looking rather like a poorly disguised tank in his camouflage fatigues, was so amazed that, in a classic double-take, he turned to the audience for an explanation (IV.ii). Mouthing his pilfered heroic phrases, John Price played Pistol as a Rocker–Rambo–Indiana Jones figure clad in black motorcycle leathers emblazoned with 'Hal's Angels' ('helter-skelter' provided the cue). His T-shirt, which read 'Never mind the bollocks; Here comes Pistol', further advertised his parodic macho prowess (Paul Brennan's Pistol imitated Dustin Hoffman's snake-eyed, double-barrelled stance in *Little Big Man* to point his aped masculinity). Indeed, 'honour' seemed to have shrunk to a single speech – Lady Percy's memory of Pistol's alter ego, Hotspur (II.iii.9-44) – and even that was undermined. When Northumberland decided to go to Scotland, Jennie Stoller's Lady stalked offstage, well aware that Hotspur was now just a name. Andrew Rissik captures a sense of how the ESC productions detailed 'the transitional agony by which one kind of governing power becomes another':

> Here ... we chart the changes in the national character, the way that society takes its cue from the personality of the man at the top. The raffish, disorderly England of ... *Part One*, with its stubborn codes of honour and obligation, gives way to a more plush and affluent world, self-centered, witty and devious, in *Part Two*. (*Plays and Players*, March 1987, p. 11)

Although that change was immediately signalled when, after pushing his wheelchair on stage, the 'crafty-sick' Northumberland nimbly settled himself in the chair with a laprobe at the sound of an offstage voice, Falstaff made it even more explicit. His first appearance was set in an elegant dining establishment where he was enjoying an after-dinner cigar (I.ii). Resplendent in a purple-and-pink-pinstripe George Melly suit that made him look like a giant fuchsia, his chest blazed with medals, which he took every opportunity to show off as proofs of his valorous service. The outrageous costume was the outward sign of a self-aggrandising vulgarity: this was a man bent on being *seen*, one who '[knew] his own worth' (Michael Billington, *Guardian*, 23 March 1987). Devoted to self-preservation at all costs, he could spin on a sixpence from the stand-up comic's ruthless mockery for the weak (including his own shortcomings) to the charming manners of the suave gent. How easily he wooed Mistress Quickly's (June Watson's) favours: an arm about her shoulders, a light caress on cheek and chin, a kiss blown delicately from his fingers and the gift of a rose, placed between her teeth (II.i). And when Shallow dredged up the tatters of their shared undergraduate past, Falstaff's faraway look and soft voice revealed, momentarily, the flickering outlines of earlier, braver days (III.ii.191-212). However much reviewers carped, either at wresting *The Henrys* to mount a critique of Thatcherite Britain or at Bogdanov's eclecticism (or at both), their praise for John Woodvine's (*The Henrys*) and Barry Stanton's (*Wars*) Falstaffs reached for superlatives:

> Woodvine glows in the part. ... He is alternately sly as a fox and warm as a coal-fire with a voice that aspires to the Silver Ring and a heart that belongs amongst the punters on the Downs. (Michael Billington, *Guardian*, 23 March 1987)

> Woodvine gives us a huge, charming George Formby of a Falstaff ... laughing a little Windsor whinny of a royal laugh – 'Haw-haw-haw' – right up in the top of his nasal passage. He has a boyish habit of canting his head to one side, and is really the sweetest old con artist – but never a buffoon. (Ray Conlogue, *Globe and Mail*, 25 May 1987)

> Pitching like a Thames barge, wearing a deckchair-striped blazer and co-respondent shoes, Woodvine's Falstaff is a classic interpretation of breadth, confidence, fastidiousness and humanity ... . The splintery, dark-etched and saturnine voice relishes every line, reference and joke as though being handed them for the first time and even more rarely he shares the delight of discovery with us without ever breaking the rhythms of the speech or scene. It must be a long time since the glorious prose-arias ... were shaped and coloured with such effortless conversational splendour. (Michael Ratcliffe, *Observer*, 28 December 1986)

> Stanton handles [Falstaff] like a Rolls he's driven all his life. He keeps buffoonery at a minimum, and doesn't even strive for wit. Like all great comics he simply describes the world as he sees it, and is appalled. (Thomas M. Disch, *The Nation*, 25 June 1988)

> Stanton's Falstaff is a monumental creation. He is as irrepressible, ridiculous and exploding with a lust for life as ever ... but the actor also shows us a man shot through with a fiercely black streak of corruption, selfishness and amorality. So when his cronies are strong-armed by the cops – and he himself is chillingly dismissed ... – it's as satisfying as watching a City Hall sleaze merchant getting his comeuppance. (Hedy Weiss, *Chicago Sun-Times*, 9 May 1988)

On the one hand, these comments focus on the actors' ability to create a psychologically convincing character; on the other, they admire both performers' consummate technical skill. It was precisely this flair for straddling the contradictions between 'the real' and 'the role' that made both these Falstaffs the source of immense pleasure. And Falstaff's own pleasures – particularly his signature obsession with drink – became the occasion for a whole range of comic inventions.

These began with a reprise of *Part One*'s drinking joke, where Falstaff had poured the remnants of five bottles into a tankard, drunk the result and proclaimed, 'I must give over this life' (I.ii.95). At Falstaff's first appearance in *Part Two*, a waiter drained five bottles of white wine into a glass, filling it to brim: Falstaff quaffed it. Then the gag expanded. In reply to Falstaff's 'What says the doctor to my water?' (I.ii.1-2), his page presented him with another wine bottle mostly full of yellow liquid; and when Falstaff absent-mindedly poured himself a glass from this bottle, he choked on the drink. Later, he offered the urine-filled wine bottle to the Chief Justice as a rare vintage: though rebuffed ('Not a penny ...' [I.ii.226]), he still had several more aces up his sleeve. Picking up the money the Justice had left on his table, he was about to leave without paying his bill when the waiter called him back. Very grandly, he paid with the stolen money, added the 'wine' as a tip and, after taking the (red) rose from the table for his lapel, left with a tiny, two-fingered wave. Here, indeed, was sterling proof of a Falstaff who could 'turn diseases to commodity' (I.ii.249-50).

To some reviewers, however, the gags were simply 'one-off effects' designed to 'create a sense of complicity between cast and audience' (Robert Hewison, *Sunday Times*, 5 January 1989). Yet since Falstaff's penchant for drink and his close relationship with the audience are grounded in Shakespeare's text, exploiting both seems justified. To be sure, the next instance, which demonstrated the results of all that drink, did more than flirt with the implications of Falstaff's 'Empty the jordan' (II.iv.33, a line Dover Wilson had urged Redgrave to underscore as an instance of the diseased realm). Writing to the Arts Minister, Mrs A. N. Butler was offended: 'We have to listen, in silence, to Falstaff relieving himself (off-stage) before he appears in the Boar's Head Tavern'; outraged that her taxes were being used to fund 'such an obscene and degrading performance,' she urged the Minister to send someone to stop 'this subversive and indecent production before further harm is done' (Bogdanov and Pennington, pp. 301-2). Falstaff's offstage action did go on and on, but rarely, one imagines, had Quickly's exquisitely timed, 'Here comes Sir John' ever drawn such knowing laughter. But perhaps the best instance of Falstaff's complicity with the audience came when, after anatomising Shallow, he pulled out a pocket flask, raised it to his lips and, acknowledging that others might share his thirst, motioned to the audience to go and have a drink as well (III.ii).

If marking the interval as a refreshment break recalled the opening restaurant joke, the Gaultree betrayal, which opened the production's second half, gave the drinking gag a more vicious turn. A smooth-faced, efficient Prince John (John Dougall) offered the rebels sherry; in the midst of their self-congratulatory toasts, commandos marched them off to execution and, with phrases from Handel echoing on the sound track ('The King shall rejoice!' 'The King shall rejoice!'), Westmoreland stayed behind, listening to the gunshots and savouring his own glass of sherry. Thus unexpected ironies surrounded Falstaff's sherris-sack speech (IV.ii.83-121), delivered in the plummy tones of a television huckster acclaiming the latest antidote for human imperfections. But if this was the final pay-off for linking drink to diseases and commodity, it was not the last of the running joke. When Shallow (Clyde Pollitt) was instructing Davy to find gourmet delights ('pigeons ..., short-legged hens, a joint of mutton, and any pretty little tiny kickshaws' [V.i.22-4]) for his guest, he held a jug of applejack. Each time he turned to Falstaff ('Sir John, you shall not be excused' [V.i.9-10]), Falstaff reached longingly for the jug; but each time Shallow turned away and poured himself another shot. Once Falstaff got the jug, it was empty; and Shallow shook a bony finger at him, as though reprimanding a naughty child. At the final Gloucestershire revel – a white-tie country dinner – everybody was smashed to the gills: Bardolph collapsed, prompting Shallow's 'Give Master Bardolph some wine, Davy' (V.iii.25); and, at Pistol's news, Shallow himself got pushed into an apple-basket and carried off at scene's end. As for Falstaff, his drinking flooded into the next play where, transformed into *Henry V*'s Chorus, he presided at stage-side, an Alastair Cooke-like figure (Woodvine in blazer and grey flannels; Stanton in tuxedo) comfortably ensconced in a swivel chair, with a brandy bottle and snifter ready to hand on a nearby table. Narrating, it would appear, had definite upmarket pay-offs.

Some gags were more insistently local. The milkmaid who urged spectators to 'Have a nice day!' (at the beginning of the first

Gloucestershire scene [III.ii]), did seem geared merely to exploit a contemporary commonplace and was eventually cut. The joke also exploited the actor, not just by using her as a medium of currency between stage and audience but by calling attention to her stereotypically domestic, nursery-tale role. Yet one could also justify such use in terms of the play, which positions its women characters as an exploited underclass. Bogdanov has said that he 'believe[s] Shakespeare was a feminist' and that 'all the plays I direct analyse ... the roles of women from that ideological point of view. I think there is no question of it: he shows how women are ill-treated [and] abused ... if they are not at the seat of power' (Holderness, *Shakespeare Myth*, p. 89). Although Bogdanov's ideas of feminism are not particularly congruent with a materialist feminist critique, the ESC production was especially alert not only to the marginal status of *2 Henry IV*'s women characters but also to the ways in which they are simultaneously victims and, like the men, victimisers. In the case of Mistress Quickly (June Watson) and Doll Tearsheet (Jenny Quayle), this contradiction was reinforced by both actors' playing style: a combination of psychological realism (which tends to enforce dominant cultural codes) borrowed from Stanislavski and a deliberate pointing of gender and class relations grounded in Brechtian techniques.

Costume gave both figures an extremely precise social and occupational coding. June Watson's Quickly wore a 'peasant' skirt, low-cut blouse and tightly fitted weskit (down-scale Laura Ashley); with the addition of a shawl and an Eliza Doolittle black straw hat (covered with mangy flowers which flopped rhythmically – 'I ... have been fobbed off, and fobbed off ...' [II.i.34-35]), she was a feistier version of *Upstairs, Downstairs*'s Mrs Bridges, and just as insistent on her rights as Falstaff was on his. Fang and Snare were at least as terrified of her as of arresting Falstaff, and with good reason, for her well-stuffed mesh shopping bag became a lethal weapon that connected with the groin of every man onstage until it was finally snatched away by Falstaff, who returned the blow to Quickly ('I'll tickle your catastrophe' [II.i.62]). When required to pay his account, Falstaff took money from her purse, at which Quickly's righteous outrage approached tears; and Falstaff, in danger of losing his next drink, quickly turned on the charm. In such a form of commodity exchange, affection becomes payment for services rendered and can stack up enormous credit. This was mutual exploitation: Falstaff aware of his dependency on Quickly for drink and credit; Quickly all too willing to take advantage of Sir John's war-hero status to collect her due.

If lower-class respectability was the touchstone of Watson's Quickly, Jenny Quayle's Doll tipped the scale in the other direction. Compared to the Lautrecian figure of Hands's production, she was even more clearly ghettoised by costume and manner. She wore a black leather bustier, mini-skirt and boots, chains and torn fishnet stockings (Francesca Ryan substituted a leopard-skin mini and punked-up hair); cheap and foul-mouthed, she carried a knife in her belt and out-Pistolled Pistol's self-display. Yet her show of putting Pistol down (the knife tickled his groin) was clearly for Falstaff's benefit; she could threaten Pistol precisely because she knew Falstaff was her protector and needed her to shore up his sexual identity. Indeed, the tavern–brothel scene (II.iv) recalled, in its mix of quarrel, interruptions and tenderness, *Part One*'s Glendower scene (III.i): both foregrounded women's presences, the Welsh lady's songs and Kate Percy's 'curses' had a down-scale echo in Doll's argot and Pistol's borrowed idioms and, at the end, both pointedly excluded women from male business. While Falstaff's upstage exit clearly prefigured his rejection, the end of the tavern–brothel scene also became an opportunity for Doll. When Bardolph summoned her to Falstaff, she adjusted her clothes, fixed her face and, accompanied by a 'Spanish' tarantella, strutted playfully off-stage in a long, long exit – a desirable (and desiring) commodity as aware of her own body as Madonna. Finally, because the production had made a point of how both women scrapped to survive, their unusually brutal arrest was especially shocking (V.iv). Both Quickly and Doll wrestled with trimly uniformed bobbies who beat Doll with nightsticks before one carried her off on his shoulder. Watching from upstage, Pistol crept away, all too willing to let 'the weaker ... emptier vessel' be the primary target of the vice squad's mopping-up operations in Eastcheap. As she was hauled off by the lackeys of Hal's new 'Christian' kingship, Quickly's 'Oh God, that right should thus o'come might' (V.iv.23-4) hung in the air. For once, it seemed, she had found precisely the right words.

III

Early on, Bogdanov and Pennington had agreed on their conception of Hal: *Part One*'s 'I know you all' plotted the arrow-straight course of a man who masked his intentions in words and became an iron-willed Henry V. Pennington explained his idea of the character's trajectory:

> What I was after for Prince Hal ... was a combination of ... chilly political clearsightedness with a wayward, unstable quality. His humour in *Henry IV* is usually based on wrong-footing those around him ... always with his intimidating blood-royalty dangerously sharpening the jokes. He is wayward in emotion, too, in that he falls dangerously in love with the life (Falstaff) that he has committed himself to leaving. There seems to be violence in his humour, in his passionate outbursts to his father, and of course in his bravery in battle – this violence becomes legalised and heroic when he becomes the implacable Warrior King, and an intemperance that had been delinquent becomes official. (Bogdanov and Pennington, pp. 49-50)

Reviewers' comments reveal an unusual match between Pennington's description of the character and his performance. Ray Conlogue called him a 'tormented, Oedipal ... nasty young man who has little capacity to care about anybody' and mentioned his 'awful smirk' and 'Puritan hatefulness' (*Globe and Mail*, 25 May 1987); Thomas M. Disch thought him 'darker, craftier, altogether more sinister' than previous Hals (*The Nation*, 25 June 1988); Andrew Rissik noted the 'slow transformation ... from calculating boy to suavely secure despot' (*Plays and Players*, March 1987). Paul Taylor, on the other hand, thought that both Pennington's Hal and his Henry V failed to come alive 'because his characterisations are calculatedly perfect studies in how to appear ambiguous at all times. Consequently, they seemed like academically excellent critiques of the parts rather than real people who are occasionally less than fully themselves' (*Independent*, 22 June 1988). Although Taylor's idea of 'life' seems tied to assumptions about Hal's 'humanity' which Pennington designed his performance to counter, he accurately identifies ambiguity as the keynote for this Hal, whose ability to exploit the moment rivalled Falstaff's.

Hal first appeared – dressed in an open-necked red shirt, cricketing trousers and plimsolls – lounging on a couch and drinking beer from a bottle (II.ii). Testy and bored, he used Poins as a whipping boy for his self-hatred, and Poins paced the room, snapping back at him. When, in reading Falstaff's letter, Hal came to 'the son of the king nearest his father' (II.ii.111-12), his bitter 'hunh' recalled the irony of the Shrewsbury rejection. The idea to go to Eastcheap came as something to do – even, perhaps, a way to feed his self-loathing further. And, as Poins started to follow Bardolph and the Page, Hal's 'Follow me, Ned' (II.ii.168) reminded him, with schoolboy condescension, of who was the leader and who the follower. When he burst in on Falstaff and Doll, he had forgotten the familiar language of insult and had to dredge it up; his attempt to reprise *Part One*'s tavern scene not only misfired but stressed his misplaced assumptions. Falstaff claimed quite honestly that he had no idea Hal was listening, and the thought that Falstaff had read through him momentarily stunned Hal. It was up to Falstaff to retrieve his princely dignity for him ('No abuse, Hal' [II.iv.327]). At the news from court, it was a deeply unsettled Hal who ripped off his drawer's apron and left, throwing 'Falstaff, good night' (II.iv.369) over his shoulder only as a half-remembered courtesy.

When he entered the chamber where his father, attended by Hal's immaculately uniformed brothers, Westmoreland and the Chief Justice, lay dying, Hal was still dressed informally, pointing the contrast between his casual attitude ('How now, rain within doors and none abroad?' [IV.iii.142]) and the others' gravity. Yet his voice broke when he thought his father dead; given this Hal's contempt for Patrick O'Connell's visionary Henry IV or for Michael Cronin's executive King who could spare him little time, his show of emotion was a surprise. But almost immediately ('My due from thee...' [IV.iii.172]) his voice changed. He reached avidly for the crown and, rising slowly, set it on his head; as though gazing into a mirror, he enjoyed the mantle of power and, hypnotised by the crown and his own image, left the room like one in a trance. As Andrew Rissik put it, 'This able and courtly gangster knows what his father perceived only in stray moments of anguish: that the crown is an idea, and that you must be intoxicated by it' (*Plays and Players*, March 1987). But if here Hal seemed to come to terms with 'lineal honour', the later crown scene reduced him to tears, and he stayed at a safe distance from his father's insults. He took them standing, knelt to apologise and, when motioned to sit by the King, curled into his father's body, both to seek its comfort and to lend his own strength to the dying man. In Michael Cronin's playing, 'And now my death / Changes the mood' (IV.iii.327-8) brought a smile; his face radiant, he spoke with the urgency of a man who was envisioning, not his son's future, but his own. He slipped into death before he could be moved to the Jerusalem Chamber, and Hal arranged his body on the bed and stood at the end, as though fixing the image in memory. From the shadows, Clarence and Gloucester entered to pull out the bed, and, to a phrase from Handel ('The King shall reign!'), Hal followed, the crown held in front of him, joining one king to another. Later, in the accession scene, his grief surfaced ('Yet weep that Harry's dead...' [V.ii.59]), only to be suppressed by Clarence's formal response ('We hope no other from your majesty' [V.ii.62]). Majesty's 'gorgeous garment', he had discovered, turned brothers to subjects, and the moment fuelled his angry attack on the Chief Justice, whose rebuke made him recognise how much he still fell short of his so recently assumed office. Naming the Chief Justice his new father brought him back to his own ('My father is gone wild into his grave' [V.ii.122]); and Pennington at first stressed the open vowels of the next few lines until, with 'to raze out / Rotten opinion' (V.ii.126-7), he began to hit each consonant, his voice growing steadily more self-assured. A king, his playing suggested, can literally make himself up out of words.

After the slowed, tipsy domesticity of Shallow's last dinner party – where space swam away into the upstage dark behind a downstage bench, a wheelbarrow and a basket of spilled apples – the staging for the royal entry, in which the two platform-trucks framed a central aisle, seemed purposefully designed to deny Falstaff a centre-stage position. As bunting and flags descended from the flies, the Gloucestershire crew assembled: Pistol wrapped in a huge Union Jack; Falstaff wearing his red-jacketed uniform and sporting a tiny bowler with a Union Jack hatband like those in Leicester Square souvenir shops. The sense of children playing at dressing-up gave a saucy undercut to the entering parade of finely dressed nobles who, to Handel's 'Coronation March', were joined by the newly crowned Henry V, his military uniform covered with an ermine-trimmed cloak. Popping in and out between the ranked nobles as though playing hide-and-seek, Falstaff called out to Hal and then knelt before him, his back to the audience. Bitterly annoyed that Falstaff had, as at Shrewsbury, interrupted yet another moment of triumph, Hal relished the dismissal. In Pennington's delivery, Hal's allowing Falstaff 'competence of life' and tendering the possibility of advancement based on reform were spoken with nastily ironic *noblesse oblige*, and he paused only long enough to make sure the Chief Justice would execute his orders.

Although a stunned Falstaff did not start to rise until 'Sir, I will be as good as my word' (V.v.83), the full impact of the rejection hit him only when everyone – even Bardolph – also turned away from him. Once again, the ESC staging quoted Welles's *Chimes at Midnight* where, in an extreme long shot, Falstaff walks slowly towards a lighted background archway, becoming increasingly diminished within the shot's deep space. Here, the Chief Justice and Prince John looked away as Falstaff passed them; but once the up-centre doors had shut him out, John turned, with a laugh, to an equally satisfied Chief Justice to praise Henry V's new regime. Empty except for these two surrogates of Henry V's authoritarian rule, the stage seemed unexpectedly still. But as they turned to go, Status Quo's 'You're in the army now' (at the top of the charts at the time) blared over the sound track, heralding the beginnings of the military action which, in the ESC's *Henry V*, would transform Agincourt into the Falklands and appropriate Shakespeare's cultural authority to interrogate a war which many have read as a present-day counterfeit of Britain's lost imperial power (see Hodgdon 1991, pp. 178-80):

> A vacation in a foreign land,
> Uncle Sam does the best he can.
> You're in the army now ...
> You'll be the hero of the neighbourhood ...

Raiding popular culture for an epilogue more analogous to *Henry V*'s closing sonnet than to *2 Henry IV*'s original Epilogue, which promises to 'continue the story, with Sir John in it, and make you merry with fair Katherine of France' (Ep. 26-7), Bogdanov's production not only called England's national destiny to account but also made contact with the wave of militarism sweeping late twentieth-century cultures. Yet the charge of that original epilogue was not entirely lost, for the ovations which greeted John Woodvine when, minus Falstaff's padding, he walked onstage as *Henry V*'s Chorus to invoke 'a muse of fire' for 'the warlike Harry' suggested that the actor, not the king, was the hero of the particular neighbourhood inhabited by the ESC.

IV

Opinion has it that, in the *Henry IV* plays, Shakespeare is most himself, most attuned to 'essential' human experience, whether that is taken to mean the dynamics of a rebellious generational quarrel between fathers and sons, the myth of royal destiny, power politics, Falstaffian wit and tavern roistering or the dodderings of a Cotswold country justice absorbed by intimations of mortality yet just as fiercely bent on upward mobility. Furthermore, the literary as well as theatrical traditions that surround the plays enclose them even more securely than any trilogy or tetralogy framework, insisting that they represent an historical past. The ESC's eclectic style certainly dusted off those layers of tradition. Where Quayle and Redgrave had relied on Tillyard's popular academic study as the basis for their staging, Bogdanov took up a resolutely anti-academic stance that favoured, to use Peter Brook's terms, 'rough' over 'deadly' theatre. Although he mentions Jonathan Dollimore's and Alan Sinfield's *Political Shakespeare* for its attention to 'the radical political subversion contained in Shakespeare's work' (Bogdanov and Pennington, p. 27), there is little sense that the contributors' analyses did more than confirm his own preconceptions about staging the plays as an encounter with present-day history. Curiously enough, the Marxism so many critics attacked is perhaps more firmly entrenched in the academy than in the realm of 'real' politics – or in the theatre. None the less, the question that surfaced repeatedly was whether Bogdanov's politics had obscured 'Shakespeare' so that he became something other than himself.

Audiences applauded, wrote thanks and threw red and white roses on the stages, but the critical establishment was more wary, and the reviews were shot through with contradictions. Clearly, critics were most at home with the Falstaffs of Woodvine and Stanton, monumental performances destined, like Quayle's, to out-live the productions of which they were such an essential part. Robin Ray, for instance, expected to carry Woodvine's Falstaff with him to the grave (*Punch*, 8 April 1987), and he was not alone. Such testimony suggests that, however updated or de-dated, Falstaff's figure remains quintessentially himself – recognisably 'Shake-spearian' whether in green smoking jacket, camouflage fatigues, or doublet and hose. Colin Farrell's Bardolph, swaying gently from side to side, accompanying Falstaff's revels with his blowsy trombone, June Watson's Quickly, and Clyde Pollitt's delightfully senile Shallow also fell into the category of recognisable Shakespeare. Yet besides those who thought the ESC 'may be the best thing to have happened to British theatre for years' (Eric Shorter, *Daily Telegraph*, 12 January 1987), others issued warnings: 'Bogdanov makes his little points about the gangsterism of the ruling class, and the eternal cynicism of politics. But the wayward diversions of his productions are not for Eng. Lit. students' (Kenneth Hurren, *Mail on Sunday*, 29 March 1987). *Punch*'s Paul Arnott was even more damning: 'By not making the effort to choose anything except the most immediate analogies and by abandoning all classicism, the

ESC lose the creative tension which arises from the enormous effort the RSC make to reach back into the past and examine the old sensibilities. 'The Wars of the Roses' is a cycle of cod history plays, full of sound and fury but, in the end, signifying nothing' (24 February 1989). Sheridan Morley concurred: 'Bogdanov's productions are aimed by the young at the young. ... Never mind the intelligence, feel the energy' (*Herald Tribune*, 2 August 1989). Such comments suggested just what was at stake in departing from literary and theatrical traditions.

Amidst the condemnations, however, there were also clear signs of change. Where with Redgrave's productions, most reviewers admired the figure of the King, described the crown scene in detail, and tied Shakespeare-history securely to ordained myths of royal culture, in the case of the ESC productions, critics made only passing mention of the three actors who played Henry IV. When reviewers did touch on the crown scene, they saw it exclusively from Hal's point of view. Admittedly, this had something to do with Pennington's 'star quality' and with firmly entrenched notions of the *Henrys* as vehicles for tracing the emergence of a 'true' King and for testing the royal hero – ingredients of one of Western civilisation's most powerfully persuasive narratives. Michael Billington, for one, was keeping Tillyard in his back pocket. He objected to Bogdanov's 'dubious Marxism' which robbed kingship of the humanity – and the historical consciousness – the plays, in his mind, were designed to celebrate (*Guardian*, 23 March 1987). Others, however, seemed more willing to suspend Tillyard and tradition and admire the ESC's liberating inventiveness. Just as the productions echoed with signs of a whole nation struggling to rethink its history, so, too, were there signs of critics struggling to rethink 'history according to Shakespeare'.

Urging readers not to miss *The Henrys*, the *Western Daily Herald*'s critic remarked, 'We shall not see their like again' (quoted in Bogdanov and Pennington, p. 62). At this writing, the borrowed words Hamlet uses to evoke his dead father have an especially prophetic ring. For the RSC's 1991 productions of *Henry IV, Parts 1 and 2*, directed by Adrian Noble, have reclaimed the plays for a more recognisable, more 'universal' Shakespeare. By contrast, Bogdanov and Pennington were well aware of shaping the *Henrys* to address a particular historical moment. They would be the first to admit that the contemporary references that infused the ESC *Henrys* with the vital energies of mass culture quickly fade. Firmly rooted in the late 1980s, such topical exhilarations were as momentary as the sound of 'face-royals', 'wassail candles', 'flap dragons', 'Althea's dream' and 'the Turk's tribute' were to audiences in 1597. Yet in playing with and on the preoccupations of a nation at an especially crucial juncture in global history, the ESC productions quite clearly affirmed the distinction between a Shakespeare who reminds us of the way we were – or would like to have been – and one that emphatically confronts us with how we are.

APPENDIX

Major actors and production staff in productions discussed

Shakespeare Memorial Theatre, Stratford-upon-Avon, 1951
Director: Michael Redgrave
Design: Tanya Moiseiwitsch and Alix Stone
Music: Leslie Bridgewater

Rumour	William Squire	*Poins*	Alan Badel
King Henry IV	Harry Andrews	*Bardolph*	Michael Bates
Henry, Prince of		*Pistol*	Richard Wordsworth
Wales	Richard Burton	*Mistress Quickly*	Rosalind Atkinson
Prince John of		*Doll Tearsheet*	Heather Stannard
Lancaster	John Gay	*Earl of North-*	
Humphrey, Duke		*umberland*	Alexander Gauge
of Gloucester	Michael Meacham	*Archbishop of York*	Robert Hardy
Thomas Duke		*Lady North-*	
of Clarence	Brendon Barry	*umberland*	Joan MacArthur
Westmoreland	Jack Gwillim	*Lady Percy*	Barbara Jefford
Earl of Warwick	Peter Jackson	*Shallow*	Alan Badel
Lord Chief Justice	Michael Gwynn	*Silence*	William Squire
Sir John Falstaff	Anthony Quayle		

Royal Shakespeare Theatre , Stratford-upon-Avon, 1975
Director: Terry Hands   Design: Farrah
Music: Guy Woolfenden   Lighting: Stewart Leviton

King Henry IV	Emrys James	*Bardolph*	Tim Wylton
Henry, Prince of		*Pistol*	Richard Moore
Wales	Alan Howard	*Mistress Quickly*	Maureen Pryor
Prince John of		*Doll Tearsheet*	Mikel Lambert
Lancaster	Charles Dance	*Earl of North-*	
Humphrey, Duke		*umberland*	Clement McCallin
of Gloucester	Stephen Jenn	*Archbishop of*	
Thomas Duke		*York*	Andre van Gysegham
of Clarence	Anthony Naylor	*Lady North-*	
Westmoreland	Reginald Jessup	*umberland*	Yvonne Coulette
Lord Chief Justice	Griffith Jones	*Lady Percy*	Ann Hasson
Sir John Falstaff	Brewster Mason	*Shallow*	Sydney Bromley
Poins	Trevor Peacock	*Silence*	Trevor Peacock

King Henry IV	Jon Finch	*Poins*	Jack Galloway
Henry, Prince of		*Bardolph*	Gordon Gostelow
Wales	David Gwillim	*Pistol*	Bryan Pringle
Prince John of		*Mistress Quickly*	Brenda Bruce
Lancaster	Rob Edwards	*Doll Tearsheet*	Frances Cuka
Humphrey, Duke of		*Earl of North-*	
Gloucester	Martin Neil	*umberland*	Bruce Purchase
Thomas Duke of		*Archbishop of York*	David Neal
Clarence	Roger Davenport	*Lady Northumberland*	Jenny Laird
Westmoreland	David Buck	*Lady Percy*	Michele Dotrice
Lord Chief Justice	Ralph Michael	*Shallow*	Robert Eddison
Sir John		*Silence*	Leslie French
Falstaff	Sir Anthony Quayle		

King Henry IV	Patrick Stewart	*Poins*	Miles Anderson
Henry, Prince		*Bardolph*	John Rogan
of Wales	Gerard Murphy	*Pistol*	Mike Gwilym
Prince John		*Mistress Quickly*	Miriam Karlin
of Lancaster	Kevin Wallace	*Doll Tearsheet*	Gemma Jones
Humphrey, Duke		*Earl of North-*	
of Gloucester	Philip Franks	*umberland*	Robert Eddison
Thomas Duke		*Archbishop of York*	John Burgess
of Clarence	Simon Templeman	*Lady North-*	
Westmoreland	Bernard Brown	*umberland*	Sheila Mitchell
Warwick	Brian Poyser	*Lady Percy*	Harriet Walter
Lord Chief Justice	Griffith Jones	*Shallow*	Robert Eddison
Sir John Falstaff	Joss Ackland	*Silence*	David Lloyd Meredith

King Henry IV	Patrick O'Connell, John Castle, Michael Cronin
Henry, Prince of Wales	Michael Pennington, John Dougall
Prince John of Lancaster	John Dougall
Humphrey, Duke of Gloucester	Charles Dale
Thomas Duke of Clarence	Martin Clunes, Stephen Jameson
Westmoreland	Michael Cronin
Lord Chief Justice	Gareth Thomas, Hugh Sullivan
Sir John Falstaff	John Woodvine, Barry Stanton

*Not all casting changes and doubles are noted here.

Poins	Charles Lawson, Charles Dale
Bardolph	Colin Farrell
Pistol	John Price, John Castle, Paul Brennan
Mistress Quickly	June Watson
Doll Tearsheet	Jenny Quayle, Lynette Davies, Francesca Ryan
Earl of Northumberland	Hugh Sullivan, Roger Booth
Archbishop of York	Darryl Forbes-Dawson, John Darrell
Lady Northumberland	Eluned Hawkins
Lady Percy	Jennie Stoller, Mary Rutherford
Shallow	Clyde Pollitt
Silence	Donald Gee, Philip Bowen

Chimes at Midnight (film), 1966

Director: Orson Welles   Costumes: Orson Welles
Cinematography: Edmond Richard   Music: Angelo Francesco Lavagnino

Henry IV	John Gielgud	*Worcester*	Fernando Rey
Prince Hal	Keith Baxter	*Northumberland*	Jose Nieto
Falstaff	Orson Welles	*Justice Shallow*	Alan Webb
Bardolph	Paddy Bedford	*Silence*	Walter Chiari
Mistress		*Pistol*	Michael Aldridge
Quickly	Margaret Rutherford	*Poins*	Tony Beckley
Doll Tearsheet	Jeanne Moreau	*Prince John*	Jeremy Rowe
Lady Percy	Marina Vlady		

*For a list of other significant twentieth-century productions of *Henry IV, Part Two*, see Scott McMillin's *Henry IV, Part One* in this series.

BIBLIOGRAPHY

Addenbrooke, David, *The Royal Shakespeare Company: The Peter Hall Years*, London, 1974.

Andrew, Dudley, *Film in the Aura of Art*, Princeton, NJ, 1984.

Auden, W. H., ' The Prince's Dog' (1948), in David Bevington, ed., *Henry the Fourth Parts I and II: Critical Essays*, New York, 1986.

Barber, C. L., *Shakespeare's Festive Comedy*, Princeton, NJ, 1959.

Barton, John, *Playing Shakespeare*, London, 1984.

Barton, John and Peter Hall, *The Wars of the Roses*, London, 1970.

Beauman, Sally (ed.), *The Royal Shakespeare Company's Production of Henry V*, Oxford, 1976.

—, *The Royal Shakespeare Company*, Oxford, 1982.

Bentley, Gerald Eades, *The Professions of Dramatist and Player in Shakespeare's Time*, 1590-1642, Princeton, NJ, 1986.

Berger, Harry, Jun., 'Sneak's Noise, or Rumour and Detextualization in *2 Henry IV*', *Kenyon Review*, 6, 1984, 58-78.

Berry, Ralph, *On Directing Shakespeare*, London, 1989.

Bevington, David, ed., *Henry the Fourth, Parts I and II: Critical Essays*, New York, 1986.

Billington, Michael, *Directors' Shakespeare: Approaches to Twelfth Night*, London, 1990.

Blau, Herbert, 'Ideology and Performance', *Theatre Journal*, 35, 1983, 441-60.

Bogdanov, Michael, and Pennington, Michael, *The English Shakespeare Company: The Story of ' The Wars of the Roses' 1986-1989*, London, 1990.

Booth, Michael R., *Victorian Spectacular Theatre 1850-1910*, London, 1981.

Bourdieu, Pierre, *Distinction*, trans. Richard Nice, Cambridge, MA, 1984.

Bradley, A. C., 'The Rejection of Falstaff,' (1902), in David Bevington, ed., *Henry the Fourth, Parts I and II, Critical Essays*, New York, 1986.

Briggs, Asa, *A Social History of England*, New York, 1983.

Bristol, Michael, *Carnival and Theater: Plebian Culture and the Structure of Authority in Renaissance England*, New York, 1985.

Brook, Peter, *The Empty Space*, London, 1968.

—, 'Style in Shakespearean Production', in Daniel Seltzer, ed., *The*

[149]

Modern Theatre: Readings and Documents, Boston, MA, 1967.

Brown, John Russell, *Free Shakespeare*, London, 1974.

Bulman, J. C., 'The BBC Shakespeare and "House Style"', in J. C. Bulman and H. R. Coursen, eds., *Shakespeare on Television*, Hanover, NH and London, 1988, pp. 50-60.

Bulman, J. C., and Coursen, H. R., eds., *Shakespeare on Television*, Hanover, NH and London, 1988.

Campbell, Lily B., *Shakespeare's Histories: Mirrors of Elizabethan Policy*, San Marino, CA, 1947.

Carlson, Marvin, *Places of Performance: The Semiotics of Theatre Architecture*, Ithaca, 1989.

Clayton, Thomas, 'Balancing at Work: (R)evoking the Script in Performance and Criticism,' in Marvin and Ruth Thompson, eds., *Shakespeare and the Sense of Performance*, Newark, DE, 1989.

Crowl, Samuel, 'The Long Goodbye: Welles and Falstaff', *Shakespeare Quarterly*, 31, 1980, 369-80.

David, Richard, 'Shakespeare's History Plays – Epic or Drama?' *Shakespeare Survey*, 6, 1953, 129-39.

—, *Shakespeare in the Theatre*, Cambridge, 1978.

Dollimore, Jonathan, and Sinfield, Alan, *eds.*, *Political Shakespeare*, Manchester, 1985.

Eagleton, Terry, *Literary Theory, An Introduction*, Minneapolis, MN, 1983.

Empson, William, ' Falstaff,' in *Essays on Shakespeare*, Cambridge, 1986.

Greenblatt, Stephen, *Shakespearean Negotiations*, Berkeley, CA, 1988.

Gurr, Andrew, *The Shakespearean Stage, 1574-1642*, Cambridge, 1980.

Hassan, Ihab, *The Postmodern Turn*, Columbus, OH, 1987.

Hayman, Ronald, *Playback*, London, 1973.

Hazlitt, William, '*Henry IV* in Two Parts' (1817), in David Bevington, ed., *Henry the Fourth Parts I and II: Critical Essays*, New York, 1986.

Hodgdon, Barbara, '*The Wars of the Roses*: Scholarship Speaks on the Stage', *Deutsche Shakespeare-Gesellschaft West Jahrbuch*, 1972.

—, *The End Crowns All: Closure and Contradiction in Shakespeare's History*, Princeton, NJ, 1991.

Holderness, Graham, ' Radical potentiality and institutional closure: Shakespeare on film and television', in Jonathan Dollimore and Alan Sinfield, *Political Shakespeare*, Manchester, 1985, pp. 202-30.

—, *Shakespeare's History*, New York, 1985.

—, (ed.), *The Shakespeare Myth*, Manchester, 1988.

Humphreys, A. R., ed., *2 Henry IV*, London, 1977.

Jameson, Fredric, 'Postmodernism, or The Cultural Logic of Late Capitalism,' *New Left Review*, 146, 1984, 53-92.

—, 'On Magic Realism in Film', *Critical Inquiry*, 12, 1986, 301-25.

Johnson, Paul, *A History of the English People*, rev. edn, New York, 1985.

Johnson, Samuel, ' Notes from the Plays of William Shakespeare' (1765), in David Bevington, ed., *Henry the Fourth Parts I and II: Critical Essays*, New York, 1986.

Jorgens, Jack, *Shakespeare on Film*, Bloomington, IN, 1977.

Kahn, Coppélia, *Man's Estate: Masculine Identity in Shakespeare*, Berkeley, CA, 1981.

Kantorowicz, Ernst H., *The King's Two Bodies: A Study in Medieval Political Theology*, Princeton, NJ, 1957.

Kowsar, Mohammad, ' Althusser on Theatre', *Theatre Journal*, 35, 1983, 461-74.

Lyons, Bridget Gellert and Dorothy Remy, eds., *Chimes at Midnight, Orson Welles, director*, New Brunswick, NJ, 1988.

McMillin, Scott, *Henry IV, Part One* (Shakespeare in Performance Series), Manchester, 1991.

Meisel, Martin, *Realisations*, Princeton, NJ, 1983.

Messina, Cedric, 'Preface' to *The BBC-TV Shakespeare: Richard II*, London, 1978.

Morris, Corbyn, ' An Essay Towards Fixing the True Standards of Wit, Humor, Raillery, Satire, and Ridicule' (1744), in David Bevington, ed., *Henry the Fourth Parts I and II: Critical Essays*, New York, 1986.

Mullaney, Steven, 'Strange Things, Gross Terms, Curious Customs: The Rehearsal of Cultures in the Late Renaisance', in Stephen Greenblatt, ed., *Representing the English Renaissance*, Berkeley, CA, 1988.

Mullin, Michael, 'Emrys James: On Playing Henry IV,' *Theatre Quarterly*, 7, 1977, 15-23.

Nashe, Thomas, *An Apology for Actors*, 1612.

Neale, Steve, 'Hollywood Strikes Back; Special Effects in Recent American Cinema', *Screen*, 21, 1980, 101-5.

O'Connor, Garry, *Ralph Richardson: An Actor's Life*, rev. edn, London, 1986.

Odell, George C. D., *Shakespeare from Betterton to Irving*, 2 vols., New York, 1966.

Plowden, Edmund, *Commentaries or Reports*, London, 1816.

Rackin, Phyllis, *Stages of History: Shakespeare's English Chronicles*, Ithaca, NY, 1990.

Rubin, Leon, *The Nicholas Nickleby Story*, London, 1981.

Saccio, Peter, 'The Historicity of the BBC History Plays', in J. C. Bulman and H. R. Coursen eds., *Shakespeare on Television*, Hanover, NH, 1988.

Smallwood, R. L., '*Henry IV, Parts 1 and 2* at the Barbican Theatre', (1983), rpt. in David Bevington, ed., *Henry the Fourth, Parts I and II. Critical Essays*, New York, 1986.

Spacks, Patricia Meyer, *Gossip*, New York, 1985.

Sprague, Arthur Colby, *Shakespeare's Histories: Plays for the Stage*, London, 1964.

Styan, J. L., *The Shakespeare Revolution*, Cambridge, 1977.

Taylor, John Russell, 'Shakespeare in Film, Radio, and Television', in J. C. Bulman and H. R. Coursen, eds., *Shakespeare on Television*, Hanover, NH, and London, 1988, pp. 11-13.

Thomson, Peter, 'Towards a Poor Shakespeare: The Royal Shakespeare Company at Stratford in 1975', *Shakespeare Survey*, 29, 1976, 151-6.

Tillyard, E. M. W., *Shakespeare's History Plays*, London, 1944.

Traub, Valerie, 'Prince Hal's Falstaff: Positioning Psychoanalysis and the Female Reproductive Body', *Shakespeare Quarterly*, 40, 1989, 456-74.

Trewin, J.C., *Shakespeare on the English Stage*, London, 1964.

Trussler, Simon, ed., *The Royal Shakespeare Company*, 1982-83, Stratford-upon-Avon, 1983.

Tynan, Kenneth, *Curtains*, New York, 1961.

Weimann, Robert, *Shakespeare and the Popular Tradition in the Theater*, Baltimore, MD, 1978.

Wells, Stanley, *Royal Shakespeare: Four Major Productions at Stratford-upon-Avon*, Manchester, 1976.

Wharton, T. F., *Text and Performance: Henry the Fourth, Parts 1 and 2*, London, 1983.

Wiles, David, *Shakespeare's Clown*, Cambridge, 1987.

Williams, Raymond, *Marxism and Literature*, Oxford, 1977.

Willis, Susan, *The BBC Shakespeare Plays: Making the Televised Canon*, Chapel Hill, NC, 1991.

Wilson, J. Dover, *The Fortunes of Falstaff*, Cambridge, 1945.

—, and Worsley, T. C., *Shakespeare's Histories at Stratford*, 1951, New York, 1952.

Yates, Frances A., *The Art of Memory*, Chicago, IL, 1966.

INDEX